BEYOND THE TETONS

Dedication

This book is dedicated to my late father-in-law,
H. W. W. "Blue Moose" Johnson (1918-1977)
who died while outfitting a trip in the Salmon
River Country, a land he loved. May his
devotion to the wilderness and the freedom it
represents live on in us all.

A Backpacking Guide to Wyoming's Teton Wilderness

BEYOND THE TETONS

RALPH MAUGHAN

PRUETT **P** PUBLISHING COMPANY
Boulder, Colorado

First Edition

1 2 3 4 5 6 7 8 9

Printed in the United States of America

Library of Congress Cataloging in Publication Data

Maughan, Ralph, 1945-
  Beyond the Tetons.

  1. Backpacking—Wyoming—Absaroka Mountains—Guide-
books. 2. Backpacking—Wyoming—Bridger National Forest
—Guide-books. 3. Backpacking—Wyoming—Teton National
Forest—Guide-books. 4. Trails—Wyoming—Guide-books.
5. Absaroka Mountains (Wyo.)—Description and travel—
Guide-books. 6. Bridger National Forest (Wyo.)—Guide-
books. 7. Teton National Forest—Guide-books. I. Title.
GV199.42.W82A375   796.5'1'09787   81-5893
ISBN 0-87108-580-1 (pbk.)   AACR2

The Teton-Washakie-Southeast Yellowstone Wilderness Complex

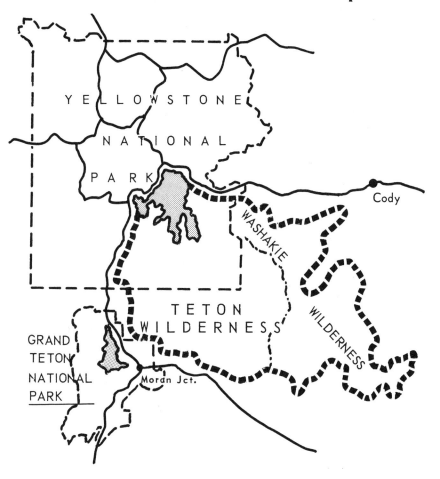

Preface

This book isn't about the Tetons. Plenty has already been written about those scenic peaks. As a result, and because they thrust their granite spires to the sky in a location where every car tourist stares, today the Tetons are crowded. You need a permit to hike their trails, and many folks have the impression from their experiences in the Tetons that all wilderness is filled to capacity.

Surprisingly, less than twenty miles away lies a huge mountain fastness, protected forever by the Wilderness Act. This area is little-traveled and hardly known except to big game hunters and a few outfitters. The place is named the Teton Wilderness. Located in the Bridger-Teton National Forest, the Teton Wilderness encompasses not the Teton Mountain Range, but rather part of the Absaroka Range and the Pinyon Peak Highlands.

The Absaroka is a dramatic range, volcanic in origin, but sculptured by ice and water. They are perhaps the wildest mountains in Wyoming. Their obscurity stems from their invisibility from the major highways. The name, "Teton Wilderness," also conspires to hide this wild country. Many people assume the Teton Wilderness must be part of the Tetons—"Oh, I was up to the Teton Wilderness last Summer too. I got a great picture of the Grand Teton. Do you want to see it?"

For some time I had wanted to visit the Teton Wilderness, depicted on most Wyoming road maps by a big blank space south and southeast of Yellowstone. At last in 1972 I was free to explore this place that showed no points of interest or filling stations on the Conoco map. I tried to get my friends to join me. At first they said yes, but then they learned the awful truth, I wasn't going to the Tetons. One-by-one, each bowed out. One bluntly told me he'd rather go somewhere exciting, not to a place no one had ever heard of. So, I made my first trip alone. Ninety miles and eight days later, I emerged at the south entrance of Yellowstone National Park. I had met only two parties during my trip.

I became entranced with this huge, but little-known wild land— its flowered meadows, broad stream valleys, box canyons with dark chasms, forested ridges, pinnacled volcanic peaks and mighty plateaus, moody tundra, wildlife and, most importantly, its deep solitude.

Since that first trip, I've returned many times. I even convinced some friends to come too. My thanks go to Lee Spradling, Jerry Jayne, Dick Farman, Margie Perez, Klaus Meier, and my wife Jackie for the company on various trips. Nevertheless, most trips were made alone.

I want to thank Buffalo District Ranger Mac Murdock for the time he spent reading this manuscript and providing information, especially since some portions of the book are critical of the U.S. Forest Service.

Thanks also go to outfitters Joe Tilden, Pete Wheeler, Jim Davis, and Joe Detimore for their information. I hope all of these men have many years of rewarding work in the mountains left to them.

Not everyone encouraged me to write this book. Many asked, "Why tell people about the place?" My answer is that wild places are being visited more not because guide books are written, but because there are more people. At the same time the undeveloped land that remains (and could be permanently preserved in the National Wilderness Preservation System) is instead being rapidly torn to shreds by timber companies, energy interests, and assorted corporate conglomerates, not to mention a new threat—the "sagebrush rebellion"—which would hand all of the public's land over to private interests. To these last groups mentioned, this book is definitely **not** dedicated.

To me, the answer is not to hide the few gems of wild country already saved, rather we should exhibit them. At the same time, we should work hard to preserve the many wild places that need legal protection. Those who want to keep the Teton Wilderness a lonely place would do well to redouble their efforts to create units of the Wilderness System in the so far untouched land in the Palisades Backcountry, the western slope of the Tetons, the Gros Ventre Range, and Lemhi Range. Otherwise, these areas will be gobbled up within five years by the energy giants, and the present-day users will end up in places like the Teton Wilderness.

Pocatello, Idaho
December, 1980

Contents

An Overview of the Teton Wilderness

Straddling the Continental Divide, just to the south and the southeast of Yellowstone National Park and the source of both the Yellowstone and the Snake River, the Teton Wilderness is almost 900 square miles in size.

Despite its immensity, it is not an isolated feature, surrounded by development on all sides. Touching it on the east is the big, lonely, and ever-so-rugged Washakie Wilderness. At its northern flank lies an unbroken expanse of wildland in famous Yellowstone. The recently established River of No Return Wilderness in Central Idaho is the only larger tract of unbroken wilderness in the United States south of Alaska.

The Teton-Washakie-Southeast Yellowstone Wilderness Complex

Mentally you can get hold of the Teton Wilderness best by thinking of it as two pieces—an eastern portion and a western portion. The eastern part is a land of high volcanic mountains and plateaus. There are great walls of rotten breccia rock and broad glacier-carved canyons with many meadows. The plateau tops are expanses of tundra with a few lakes and many ponds. During snow melt many waterfalls drop from the plateau tops to the forest and meadows below. These volcanic plateaus are the Absaroka Mountains which rise to 12,165 feet in the Teton Wilderness at Younts Peak. Further east in the Washakie Wilderness lies the 13,153 foot Francs Peak.

The western part of the Wilderness is more subtle. Soft sedimentary rocks, formed in ancient seas, underlie this area. It is a land of ridges, canyons, and stream valleys known as the Pinyon Peak Highlands. Here one finds many shallow ponds, and (at a lower elevation than in the Absarokas) a few substantial lakes, and many splashing creeks that tumble from their sources in the forested ridgetops. While less dramatic than the Absarokas, the landscape here is more complex.

All of the Teton Wilderness is characterized by flower-filled meadows and grassy slopes that break up the forest.

The Teton Wilderness is more variable than Yellowstone in all but hot springs, of which there are none. I think it is more interesting to travel through than Yellowstone's backcountry.

Perhaps the best thing about this country is its immensity and lack of crowding. It is common to walk for several days, even a week, and not see another soul. Only the Pacific Creek Trail, the lower parts of the North and South Buffalo River, Yellowstone Meadows, and the area around Thorofare Creek, could be considered busy. The Teton Wilderness is a great contrast to the Teton Mountains, the Sawtooths and much of the Wind River Range, where you can easily pass 30-40 other people in a day. Visitor use in 1976 was only a third as much as the Grand Teton National Park backcountry, and yet the Teton Wilderness is about three times as large. This means only about one tenth as many people use each acre in the Teton Wilderness as opposed to the overcrowded Tetons. Furthermore, the topography of the Teton Wilderness allows its visitors to spread out more, and thus be less visible to each other.

In recent years, the use of many units of the National Wilderness Preservation System has exploded. This hasn't happened to the Teton Wilderness. Estimated visitor-days in 1980 were about the same as 15 years earlier. Most people come in July and August with quite a few hunters using it also in September and October.

Wildlife

The Teton Wilderness is the best place in Wyoming to see big game, second only to Yellowstone and Grand Teton National Parks. Unlike the two parks, hunting is allowed (as it is in all national forests).

Moose, elk, and deer are very common. Bighorn sheep roam the high plateaus and ply the craggy summits in the Absarokas. The sheep are especially abundant on the Thorofare Plateau. Coyotes are very common. Their mournful howl is heard on many nights. There are a few mountain lion, and recent reports indicate that the wolverine and the Rocky Mountain Wolf are both returning to the area. Unfortunately, recent political changes in Washington will probably mean a return to indiscriminate predator poisoning, perhaps once again eliminating these two wilderness beasts.

There are a lot of bear. This includes the magnificent grizzly. I feel I should say a good deal about the grizzly here, both because of its rugged beauty and because of its potential threat to humans.

It is estimated that about 45 grizzlies inhabit the Bridger-Teton National Forest. Most of these are in the Teton Wilderness, although an occasional bear ventures as far south as the Gros Ventre River. Most recent estimates are that from 180 to 350 grizzlies live in the entire Yellowstone ecosystem, which includes Yellowstone Park, the Teton Wilderness, the North Absaroka Wilderness, the Washakie Wilderness, the Beartooth Wilderness, and unclassified forest land on the Targhee and Gallatin National Forests west and northwest of Yellowstone Park. From this, you can see that the Teton Wilderness is among the prime grizzly areas in the entire Yellowstone area. However, in the eight years I have visited the Teton Wilderness, I have yet to spot a grizzly or be bothered by one in camp at night. I have run into them several times, however, in the other wildernesses adjacent to Yellowstone and in Yellowstone, itself.

By and large, the grizzlies of the Teton Wilderness seem to be well behaved. No one has ever been killed or mauled by one there. However, a number of outfitters have had their cook tents demolished and a few years ago several pack horses were killed when left unattended with fresh elk kills on their backs. Thus, there seems to be no need for great concern, but you should be careful.

Grizzlies have been reported in all parts of the Teton Wilderness, but a ten-year inventory of sightings indicates that the following areas have the highest concentrations of grizzly bears: Fox Park, Yellowstone Meadows, the Soda Fork of the Buffalo, the upper North Fork of the Buffalo, Brown's Meadows, and Two Ocean Pass.

Outfitters, with their semi-permanent camps, bacon-smoked cook tents, and big game kills in the Fall, have almost all of the trouble. However, I would not be telling the truth to say that the backpacker or the equestrian is totally safe. To me, however, a tolerable level of danger is part of the wilderness experience. You could do worse than be killed by a grizzly, and most of us will do worse—cancer, emphysema, heart disease.

If you do the following, your chances of a grizzly story will be nil. First, don't camp on or next to a trail. Bears and other animals use them at night. The grizzly is most active at night. Anyway, Teton Wilderness regulations prohibit camping within 200 feet of a trail. Likewise, don't wander up and down the trails at night.

Don't cook right next to your tent or pour grease onto the ground. Pour it carefully into the fire. Don't keep food in your tent. Stuff it in a bag and hang it suspended from a tree branch with a nylon cord. It should be at least ten feet off the ground and four feet from the tree trunk. It should also be a foot or two below the branch from which it is suspended.

Don't bring bacon. Bears love it and seemingly can smell it for miles.

While somes are good bear dogs, your pet is more likely to be a danger to you than a help. This is what may happen. Your dog will run down the trail ahead of you and meet a bear. Bears hate barking dogs. The bear will chase the dog, and guess what the dog will bring along behind it as it seeks safety by its master?

If you are traveling alone or with just one other person, you could surprise a bear, and they don't like surprises. The worst situation is to meet a sow with her cubs.

If you do meet a grizzly, don't run. Stand your ground. Running excites a grizzly. Talk to the bear in low, soothing tones. If the bear stands up, it doesn't mean doom to you. They don't see well; it is probably trying to get a better look at what you are. Move slowly and laterally away from the bear. If the bear charges, lay down and play dead. Often they will stage a mock charge. Even if the bear does charge, chances are you'll get sniffed and maybe pawed around just a little bit.

If a tree is close, climb it. Grizzlies can't climb, or at least not very high.

Note: The beauty of the country may set your pulse racing. So may the attractiveness of your companion, but bears seem to be attracted by human sexual activity. It's hard to say if they are lecherous and want to watch or have enrolled in the Moral Majority and want to punish. I wouldn't have sex in heavy bear country, regardless of the bears' motive.

I hope this lecture on bears hasn't scared you, but if it has, I guess those who felt this book would cause a stampede of visitors to the Teton Wilderness can breathe a sigh of relief.

The grizzly bear, by the way, has been placed on the threatened species list. This has prevented all (legal) hunting of them in the national forests surrounding Yellowstone Park. Some question the wisdom of this policy. They say that bears are more wary of humans if they have a bullet put near them once in a while. It's hard to say. The real problem, however, isn't the person with the gun. The grizzly is a wilderness animal; it just can't adjust to development—new resorts, roads, ski areas, timber cutting, mines, oil and gas development, and people who can't walk anywhere and need a rip-roaring machine to ride are the real danger to the grizzly's future.

The National Park Service and the Forest Service relocate grizzly bears that have lost their fear of man or have begun to habituate developed campgrounds or other areas of human concentration. Hopefully this procedure will help preserve the grizzly, even as their habitat continues to shrink. I just thought you might want to know, the following places in the Teton Wilderness are where the Park Service or the Forest Service relocates the "bad" bears: the Thorofare Plateau, the Buffalo Plateau, Two Ocean Plateau, Mountain Creek, and Coulter Creek. Just because bears are relocated to these spots doesn't mean they'll stay there. Some do. Others may travel to another spot miles away in a hurry—often back to where they were captured.

Another dangerous animal is the moose—the largest of the deer family. Moose are big, fast, and unpredictable. I was chased by a big bull moose at Terrace Meadows on the South Fork of the Buffalo in Autumn 1973. The bull moose are dangerous during the autumn rut, but cow moose with calves can be a danger all year long. Detour around moose. They may look ungainly to you, but their speed is incredible—even through dense, deadfallen timber. The best places to find moose are in Arizona Creek, Pilgrim Creek, the Yellowstone Meadows, around Enos Lake, and Pendergraft Meadows. However, they can be found anywhere in the Teton Wilderness.

The most abundant big game animal in the Wilderness is the elk. The famous Jackson Hole elk herd summers largely within the Teton Wilderness. Elk favor the tops of the plateaus and the ridgelines. The Thorofare, Buffalo, and Two Ocean Plateaus, plus Big Game, Wildcat, Kitten, Bobcat and Huckleberry Ridges, allow you to see large herds. Elk are wary, however, and despite their abundance, it is hard to get close to them on a regular basis.

While not as abundant as the elk, mule deer are common in the Teton Wilderness and easy to see. The deer favor the lower elevations where aspen and cottonwood trees are mixed in with the conifers. Unfortunately, most of the deer of the Teton Wilderness are doomed. They can't survive the deep snows of the Wilderness and most migrate south into Jackson Hole. Their Winter range in Jackson Hole and the Snake River Canyon further south is being subdivided at a rapid rate. Starvation and killings by domestic dogs are rapidly depleting the ranks of these poor animals that migrate out of the Wilderness to find their tiny winter's home covered by the works of a fast-buck subdivider.

The elk at Jackson Hole are fed hay on the National Elk Refuge, so they can survive; but deer can't eat hay very well. They often starve to death with their bellies full of hay. The few deer that will survive in the Teton Wilderness are those that migrate into the Washakie Wilderness, thence to winter grounds to the northeast.

The plight of the deer in Jackson gives a lesson in conservation politics. A few years ago, Teton County, Wyoming came up with a comprehensive plan for the private land in the county that would preserve open space and wildlife habitat, while encouraging orderly economic growth. Soon, however, the county commission was taken over by a band of developers and the comprehensive plan, bit-by-bit, was out the window. If the 1982 election brings a return to orderly growth and conservation, it will probably be too late to correct the damage. In conservation, you just can't afford to lose elections because development is permanent.

What about moose winter range? Fortunately, moose can survive in the deep snow of the Teton Wilderness or in Grand Teton National Park.

Fishing

Fishing in the Teton Wilderness is very good. Many of the waters not only have abundant numbers of fish, but large ones as well. The native fish are the cutthroat trout and the mountain whitefish. These have been supplemented with rainbow, brook, and golden trout, and, in Enos Lake, Utah Chub, a trash fish.

The fishing is best in the dramatic scenery of the Wilderness' eastern half. This accounts in part for the greater visitor use on the east half of the Wilderness. Most superlative is the Yellowstone River, Thorofare Creek, and Bridger Lake. In these areas it is hard to catch a trout under 14 inches. Open Creek, Pacific Creek, the three forks of the Buffalo River, Enos Lake, Crater Lake, the Angle Lakes, and the unnamed lakes at the south foot of the Cub Creek Plateau offer good fishing too. Above timberline on the vast Buffalo Plateau sits Ferry Lake. It contains hard-to-catch golden trout.

In 1977 I led a young man from Germany into the Thorofare Country. I'll bet he thought he'd never reach fishing waters after the 4000 foot, 21-mile struggle out of Deer Creek, and down Butte Creek to Thorofare Creek. But on his first cast at Thorofare Creek, he caught a 16 inch cutthroat. From there on, he landed about five similar-sized trout an hour.

Fishing in the Teton Wilderness is regulated by the Wyoming Department of Game and Fish. You need a Wyoming fishing license. The fishing just northward in Yellowstone Park is fabulous, especially in the remote southeast corner of the Park. Yellowstone Park rules require a free Yellowstone Park fishing permit. Even though the permit is free, you'd better have it with you or you could be fined.

Weather

You should always be prepared for rain if you plan to stay overnight, not that the Wilderness is terribly damp, but because the weather is unpredictable. Getting wet ten miles from the road is unpleasant and sometimes dangerous. Some summers it will not rain for two or three weeks. Other times it will rain off and on every day for several weeks, especially during August. These rains are rarely continuous. Steady rain for more than two days is rare, but a procession of short, six or seven a day, thunderstorms can take place for a week or more.

The weather on the generally trailless, high plateaus of the Wilderness is often severe. Keep off of these vast expanses of tundra when clouds are gathering. There are few places up there to hide from lightning, and you often can't get off the plateaus due to miles of rimrock on their edges. Because you can get lost on the relatively featureless plateaus on a clear day, consider what problems you would have in a drizzle or snowstorm (it snows at least a bit every month of the year on the plateaus). Summer snow melts quickly, however.

June

June is usually a wet month. Rains of several days are more common then. Even in sunny years, the meadows are still very wet. Snow persists above about 9000 feet. Many of the lower trails are passable, however. The biggest hindrance is the stream crossings. Most of the larger streams are impossible throughout June, and there are few bridges in the Teton Wilderness. Mosquitos emerge in mid-June. With all of the wet meadows, they can be vicious, although I don't think they are as bad as the mosquitos in the Wind River Mountains.

Despite the disadvantages, there are many nice things about June in the Teton Wilderness. The Absarokas are topped with white. Ephemeral waterfalls and cascades tumble from their volcanic walls. The ridges of the western wilderness look like green velvet with the new growth. Wildlife is easier to see, and visitors are very scarce.

July

July is the driest month of the year. It is also the hottest with temperatures sometimes climbing to eighty. The streams are most beautiful in July. No longer in flood, they are clear and yet still very full. Mosquitos are bad throughout most of July, and the warmer weather allows them to be active throughout more of the night.

Late July is the time when the flowers are at their peak, although flowers bloom in the Teton Wilderness from early June until mid-September.

August

August is the month with the heaviest use. The weather is usually a bit damper than July's. Thunderstorms become more numerous and, by the end of the month, a brief snow is possible on land below the plateau tops. Even small thunderstorms can produce violent winds and large hail is commonplace. You should not seek refuge under a stand of lodgepole pine in a thunderstorm. You will notice that there is usually a jungle of fallen logs under a stand of lodgepole. This didn't happen in some cataclysm during the misty past. Lodgepole are very shallow-rooted, and some topple with every wind. Once in Arizona Creek, one fell less than fifty yards from me on a day that was completely still. It is smart not to camp under these trees.

The mosquitos recede in August, only to be replaced by biting flies. These vary from small to large. The deer flies are the worst. They land on you only to fly off with a chunk of your flesh. Fortunately, the cooler days or windy days keep these rascals at bay.

September

September is cool in the day and quite cold at night. The bugs are gone and so are most of the flowers. A few showy asters may remain. Often new snow coats the peaks, making a beautiful picture when shot through a frame of golden aspen leaves. You should be prepared for cold weather and snow, although the snow will seldom fall deeper than four or five inches and usually melts. Mid-September is hunting season, and the trails are quite busy with outfitters guiding those who seek a quality hunt.

Winter

The western wilderness is fine country for ski touring. Solitude is absolute. No one else is seen and the whine of snowmobiles will not be heard. You are likely to see wintering moose and elk. Please give them plenty of room as they have little energy to spare running from you. Many never make it through the long winters.

The snow depth in the Teton Wilderness and the southeast part of Yellowstone is probably the greatest of any place in Wyoming.

Fire and Wilderness

A unit of the National Wilderness Preservation System such as the Teton Wilderness is something more than a backcountry recreation area where no roads or vehicles are allowed. These lands are managed to perpetuate their natural state, and in recent years foresters have come to realize that true wildland has periodic fires. If fire is completely eliminated from a forest, several undesirable changes will occur. First, the meadows will gradually fill up with trees. Second, sun-loving trees like aspen and lodgepole pine will die and be crowded out by climax forest, which in the Teton Wilderness usually means spruce and Douglas fir. Third, natural fires tend to remain small even without control efforts, but if many years pass without a fire there is a large build-up of dead wood and the likelihood of a huge and catastrophic fire increases greatly. Finally, conversion of the land to deep climax forest reduces the number of most types of big game animals the land can support.

With the above in mind, the Forest Service and the National Park Service were experimenting with letting fires started by lightning burn themselves out. For the past several years, most naturally caused fires have been allowed to burn in the Teton Wilderness and in Yellowstone National Park. Visitor-caused fires were suppressed as before. Unfortunately, just as this ecologically enlightened policy that would maintain wildlife habitat and the beautiful mosaic of forest and meadow was taking hold, interference from politicians put a temporary end to the program in the Teton Wilderness.

In 1979 a natural fire on the Targhee National Forest, 150 miles west in Idaho, was allowed to burn 30,000 acres because the damage it was doing was nil, but the cost of extinguishment would have been extraordinary. In fact, the Forest Service had been burning patches in the area each Fall on purpose to create more range for livestock and habitat for wildlife. When the fire was finally controlled as a change in the weather made control possible, Idaho's Governor caused such a stink about the forest land that had been "destroyed" that the Forest Service abandoned their natural burn policies nationwide. Hopefully, in a few years a careful policy of letting natural fires burn will be restored for the Teton Wilderness.

How to Get to the Teton Wilderness

Despite its size, road access to the edge of the Teton Wilderness is good. Only the Pilgrim Creek trailhead is difficult to reach.

U.S. 89/287 and U.S. 26/287 closely approach the western and southern portions of the Wilderness for many miles. The Pilgrim Creek, Pacific Creek, and Brooks Lake roads are dirt spurs that lead to the trailheads from this all weather highway. The Buffalo Valley Road is a paved secondary road that leaves U.S. 26/287 about four miles east of Moran Junction. It provides easy access to the Lava Creek, Box Creek, Clear Creek, and Buffalo River trails. The Sheffield Creek, Arizona Creek, and Angles trailheads are almost on the main highway.

The trailheads vary greatly in the amount of use they receive. Busiest is the Turpin Meadows trailhead. This provides access to the North and South Buffalo River trails. It's quite crowded. Following it, in descending order of use, are the Pacific Creek trailhead, Brooks Lake, Angles, Box Creek, Sheffield Creek, Pilgrim Creek, Clear Creek, Arizona Creek, and Lava Creek. The last five are so little-used that two cars at the trailhead is exceptional. The Angles trailhead was recently improved. Itsprovides easy access to the popular South Fork of the Buffalo River, and its use is growing rapidly.

The Teton Wilderness can also be entered on many routes from the north and the east. These require long hikes through Yellowstone Park or the Washakie Wilderness. Many of these trails have great beauty. The most popular one, and the only one which is used primarily to enter the Teton Wilderness, is the Deer Creek trailhead. It begins on the South Fork of the Shoshone River and climbs 4000 feet in 10 miles through the Washakie Wilderness before reaching the Teton Wilderness boundary.

Maps

The entire Teton Wilderness and the adjacent Washakie Wilderness are covered by topographic maps of the U.S. Geological Survey. In addition, there exist geological maps showing the surface geology of the Huckleberry Mountain, Mt. Hancock, and Two Ocean Pass quadrangles.

The U.S.G.S. topographic maps are mostly quite recent, with the exception of three quadrangles available only in the 1:62,500 scale. These three older (and poorer) maps are Huckleberry Mountain, Mt. Hancock, and Two Ocean Pass. There are some errors on all the maps, however, even on the newest of the 1:24,000 scale quadrangles.

U.S. Forest Service photo.

Meadows of Thorofare Creek as viewed looking eastward near the mouth of Open Creek.

Almost all of these errors are minor fortunately, consisting mostly of showing trails that don't exist, failing to show ones that do exist, or showing the wrong location of trails.

The Forest Service will provide you with a basic recreation map of the Teton Wilderness for fifty cents or one of the Buffalo, Hoback, and Gros Ventre Ranger Districts for $2.00. The Teton Wilderness is located on the Buffalo Ranger District, and the $2.00 map is the more accurate of the two. Neither map is suitable for trail or cross country use, however. You absolutely should not enter a part of the Teton Wilderness you haven't entered before without the topographic quadrangle of that area. The Teton Wilderness is big and deep. Many parts are densely covered by timber and have no prominent landmarks. In the western half of the Wilderness, many trails are poor, seldom-used, and can be confused with game trails. Furthermore, if you do get lost the old idea that following a stream will lead you back to civilization doesn't hold. Here, it is more likely to lead you down into a gorge, to the lip of a waterfall, or further from people into the Washakie Wilderness or the Yellowstone National Park backcountry.

Trails of the Teton Wilderness

About 500 miles of trails await the adventurer in the Teton Wilderness. The precise mileage is indefinite because some are vague and are maintained only by outfitters. This book describes the large majority of the trails, but a few abandoned or outfitter trails are excluded.

About eighty per cent of the trail traffic is on horses—mostly folks being guided in by outfitters. This makes the heavily-used trails a bit smelly, but on most trails horse manure isn't a problem simply due to the low use they receive. Undoubtedly some will complain about the horses, but please remember that these outfitters make their living in the Wilderness. They generally take good care of the country. Most importantly, they expose the lie told by the developers and their kept politicians that Wilderness is a lock-up of resources, used only by the hardy backpacker, and that Wilderness protection means poverty. Most of the outfitters make a fine living—a good deal better than loggers or miners.

The trails in the eastern half of the Wilderness tend to be obvious and well-signed. The opposite is true in the lonely western portion. You can expect to spend some time holding the map and puzzling over the identity of faint tracks in the forest. These faint trails can be accurately followed for many miles if you know how and are careful. Here are some pointers.

Look for blazes cut into the tree trunks. The route of many trails is marked by frequent blazes. These blazes, probably first cut by army crews in the late 1800s, look like an upside down exclamation point. They are usually located on the oldest, and therefore, the biggest trees.

You can use the blazes to follow a trail route even when the track or tread has disappeared completely. In fact, that's the purpose of a blaze.

With lack of use, the track of a trail disappears rapidly in a meadow. On many trails you will find that the trail fades out at each meadow. This makes it crucial to look for a blaze marking the trail when you reach the meadow's other side. In contrast, a track remains for a long time on the forest floor because grass and shrubs fill it in very slowly. Many such tracks exist in most stretches of forest in the Teton Wilderness. Unfortunately, most of the tracks are game trails. So once again, look for the track with a blaze.

Most Teton Wilderness trails go either upstream or downstream. If you lose the trail, you can usually pick it up by angling upslope from the stream or downslope to the stream.

When you are planning a trip, there are a number of things to consider in selecting a trail (besides its length and to where it leads).

First of all, what condition is the trail in? A trail in poor condition will be slower. You have to consult the map frequently, step over logs, and maybe walk through damp areas.

Second, how much does the trail climb? Long ascents, or trails with numerous ups-and-downs, take energy beyond the number of miles on the trail signs.

Third, is the maximum altitude on the trip commensurate with the ability of the party and the weather? Some people can get altitude sickness above 9000 feet. The temperature drops and the wind increases with altitude. The ultraviolet radiation from the sun is much more intense on the plateaus of the Teton Wilderness than down in the stream valleys. Climbing 500 feet is harder on a trail that is already at 9500 feet than down at 7500 feet near the trail's start.

Fourth, what kind of river crossings are there? There are a number of large streams in the Teton Wilderness, and yet only three bridges in the entire area. It is frustrating to begin a fifty-mile loop trip and then discover after walking thirty miles there is a river you cannot cross.

Finally, how much solitude is there? Here as elsewhere, wilderness travelers tend to gang up on certain attractions. If you want solitude foremost, go up Lava Creek, for instance, rather than heading straight to Yellowstone Meadows like so many others do. Fortunately, most of the trails in the Teton Wilderness are very lightly used.

In the trail descriptions that follow, I have indicated the trail's length, its general condition, the amount of use it gets in the Summer, the miles of effort required, the number of stream crossings of substance on the trail, and the earliest date the average backpacker can make the crossing. Horses can make most of these crossings a week or two earlier.

In general, for every five hundred feet you climb, you use as much energy as if you walked an additional mile on the level. This is how I calculated the effort-miles. As a general guide to the amount of trail use, I have used the following categories: very light (one party a week or less); light (one party every other day); medium (one or two parties a day); heavy (more than two parties a day). By these standards even a heavily used trail may seem uncrowded when compared to the trails of other wilderness areas.

Description of the Trails

1 SHEFFIELD CREEK
(also called Huckleberry Ridge)

Length: 12 miles.
Effort: 16½ miles from trailhead to Brown's
    Meadow; 13½ miles from Brown's
    Meadow to trailhead.
Trail condition: Fair to poor.
River crossings: One at trailhead, June 25.
Trail use: Light.
Topographic Quadrangle: Huckleberry
    Mountain.

Called the Sheffield Creek Trail on the maps, but the Huckleberry Ridge Trail on the trail signs, you reach this trailhead by turning onto a dirt road on the east side of U.S. 89/287 just 2.7 miles south of Yellowstone Park's south entrance. This dirt road is immediately south of the highway bridge spanning the Snake River at Flagg Ranch—a busy tourist stop.

The road ends after 0.3 miles. There is an improved trailhead

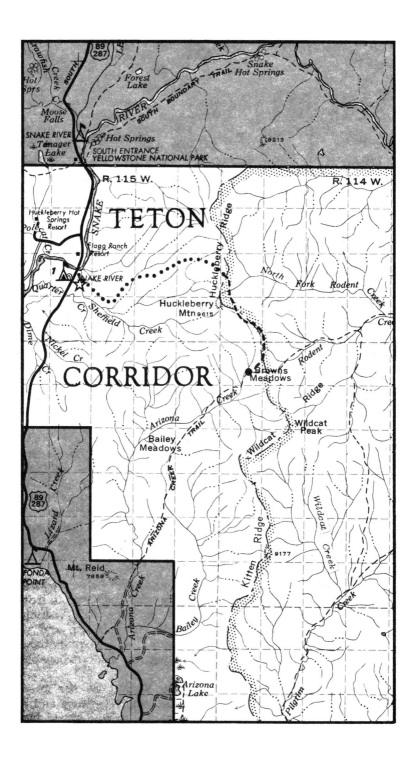

here right at the ford of Sheffield Creek. Wade across willow-lined Sheffield Creek, and then follow a jeep trail 0.1 miles to a fork. Take the right fork. This heads across a small meadow to a sign which reads "Huckleberry Ridge Trail." Gird your loins for the beginning of a nearly continuous climb of 2200 feet to the top of Huckleberry Ridge. The climb begins just past the sign. You may wish to remain a while and fish in the meadow for the small cutthroat trout in the creek.

The trail ascends 1600 feet without a break. Finally, there is a short descent across the head of Sheffield Creek. The top of Huckleberry Ridge is a climb of 600 more feet, passing through scattered open forest with a beautiful view of the northern portion of the Teton Range. On top, at 9200 feet, the Tetons lie before you to the west and southwest. To the northwest is the flat, forested Pitchstone Plateau in Yellowstone Park, formed just yesterday (in geologist's time) by vast outpourings of lava.

Snowdrifts linger on the seven-mile-long top of Huckleberry Ridge until mid-July. Winter storms leave over 300 inches of snow here a year. But by mid-August, the tributaries of Sheffield Creek encountered on the trail have largely gone dry. You should bring water for this long and rewarding climb.

Huckleberry Ridge is a place for cross-country hiking. While not exactly a level walk, the ridgetop isn't hard to traverse from its beginning at Arizona Creek northward to its terminus in Yellowstone. Here in Yellowstone, you look down on the Snake River far below. The volcanic Red Mountains rise just to the North.

Descending the back side of Huckleberry Ridge, you ramble through open and flowery slopes and patches of forest. You can see down Rodent Creek (a pretty place despite its name) and North Rodent Creek to the heavily-forested primeval wilderness in Coulter Creek. On the eastern horizon is massive and hard to reach Big Game Ridge. Southward is the sharp profile of Wildcat Peak, with some of its namesake in the general area.

At the start of the descent into Rodent Creek, a trail leaves to the left. This is a non-maintained shortcut to the Rodent Creek Trail (Trail 2b). Just a little further is a trail to the right, leading to the top of Huckleberry Mountain. At 9615 feet, this short spur places you on the highest point on Huckleberry Ridge; and here is a rustic old fire lookout.

From here the trail drops about 900 feet to Brown's Meadow—a beautiful place at the top of Rodent Creek. This is the juncture of many trails. At the edge of Brown's Meadow the trail forks. The right fork leads past a very unsightly outfitter's cabin (a veritable junk pile in the wilderness) and to the Arizona Creek Trail (Trail 2). The left fork leads to the Rodent Creek Trail and past an old grave. The faint, weathered inscription on this wooden cross reads, "T. Brown 1881." Little is known about Brown, but I sensed his soul was at rest as I sat by his grave late one afternoon and watched the elk cautiously emerge from the forest to graze on his peaceful meadow. The mood can change fast. As night descended, the increasing numbers of dark shapes on the meadow made tranquility fade. I retreated to the warmth of my fire at camp. Brown's Meadow gets more than its share of grizzly bears.

Brown's Meadow is the only place to camp on the Sheffield Creek Trail. There is too much slope and not enough water on the rest of the trail for an adequate campsite.

The top of Huckleberry Ridge and the middle of Brown's Meadow mark the western boundary of the Teton Wilderness. The land west of the boundary, but east of the highway, constitutes what is called the Teton Corridor. The Corridor has been proposed for classification as part of the Teton Wilderness by the Forest Service. The only opposition seems to be from the oil lobby, but that is powerful. Until Congress decides the question, the Corridor is being managed as though it were part of the Teton Wilderness.

2 ARIZONA CREEK

Length: 8½ miles.
Effort: 12 miles.
Trail condition: Fair.
River crossings: Two, July 10.
Trail use: Very light.
Topographic Quadrangles: Colter Bay,
*   Huckleberry Mountain.*

All of the Arizona Creek trail lies outside of the Teton Wilderness, but inside of the Teton Corridor proposed wilderness addition or else in Grand Teton National Park. It passes through very wild country, and the trail gets very little use.

The trailhead is a short distance off of U.S. 89/287. Take the obscure dirt road that heads eastward at a point immediately north of the highway bridge (unsigned) over Arizona Creek. The dirt road is not signed, but it is exactly 4.8 miles north of the Colter Bay Village side road.

The dirt road ends after about 100 yards at a corral. Here a log blocks further vehicular passage. Park your car and walk for about 50

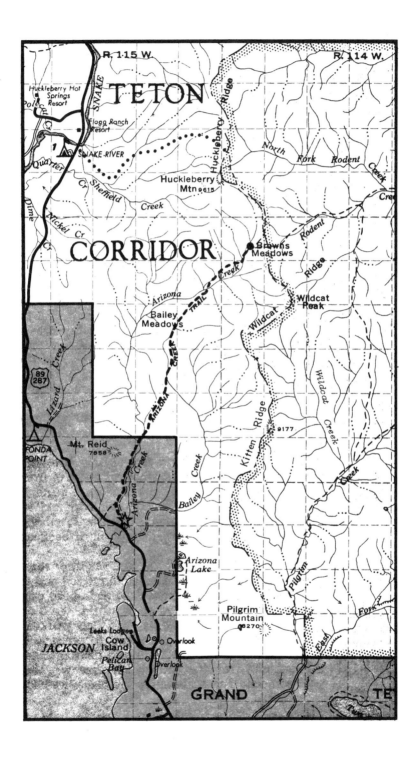

The Tetons and Jackson Lake from top of Kitten Ridge.

yards down this barred road to a second corral. From here an un-signed path leads into the woods on the corral's left side. You should note that the USGS Colter Bay topographic quadrangle incorrectly shows a primitive road going up Arizona Creek for about a mile. This was true in the past, but the road has been closed for some time. It is rapidly reverting to nature.

The faint, unsigned path is the start of the Arizona Creek Trail. I saw a pine marten here, evidence of undisturbed wilderness country. The path winds through a short stretch of lodgepole pine woods. Then it breaks into a meadow. The meadow is large and pleasant, but the noise of the highway traffic intrudes as do the powerlines toward which the trail heads and passes under. Past the powerlines, the trail climbs through aspen and into a thick stand of lodgepole as you cross over a gentle hill and drop slowly down to Arizona Creek. The sounds of the machine culture fade—deep wilderness lies ahead.

The north end of the Tetons from Bailey Meadows.

Arizona Creek meanders gracefully amid open forest and thick willows. The creek looks like good fishing. It has nice holes, but there are lots of big suckers crowding out the trout. The willows and forest near the creek are full of moose, coyotes, elk, deer, and bear (some grizzly). You would do well to make some noise as you walk. I've been through twice and surprised moose on the trail both times.

The first ford of Arizona Creek has a gentle current, but it is fairly deep until mid-Summer. Three-fourths of a mile past this ford, a metal stake in the ground marks the passage from Grand Teton National Park to the Bridger-Teton National Forest. Hopefully, some day soon it will also be the western boundary of the Teton Wilderness.

Soon the trail forks at an unsigned junction in a small meadow. The left fork is a fisherman's trail. It continues a short distance up this wild stream valley. The valley narrows to a tight canyon and travel upstream ceases. You take the right fork, which soon enters forest and climbs 700 feet up the ridge to the east. The climb ends at a long pretty meadow through which runs Bailey Creek. While small here, Bailey Creek is a major tributary of Arizona Creek, with about two miles of fishing further down the meadow. Interestingly, there is a small flammable gas seep in the meadow.

Kitten Ridge is the eastern side of the meadow. It is a steep, but beautiful, cross country hike to its top. Elk are numerous up there, and you get a premier view of the Tetons.

The trail cuts diagonally across the northern end of this grassy subalpine meadow, and Bailey Creek is crossed with a small jump. The creek is entrenched deeply into a tiny slot in the meadow sod, about six feet down.

At the end of the meadow, you enter forest with many small openings filled with bluebell and forget-me-nots. Be careful not to follow a game trail. There are many that leave the trail. You climb gently about 300 feet and then descend 300 feet to the upper crossing of Arizona Creek. Being a northwest-facing slope, this part of the trail is very damp. Sometimes it is almost a quagmire. The trail passes through a dense climax forest of spruce and fir. I've seen many bear tracks in this section. The air is that of absolutely raw wilderness.

The upper crossing of Arizona Creek isn't deep; but it is swifter than the lower crossing, with the total water flow being about the same. After this ford, you climb steeply about 500 feet over the southernmost flank of Huckleberry Ridge, with its large volcanic cliffs looming overhead. On this section of trail, you cross many small streams. These are not shown on the USGS topographic quadrangle.

The trail ends at the edge of Brown's Meadow where the headwaters of Arizona Creek tumble from that scenic elk pasture into a canyon. Here, by the junk cabin, you can pick up many other trails.

2a BROWN'S MEADOW TO WILDCAT DIVIDE

Length: 2 miles.
Effort: 3 miles.
Trail condition: Fair.
River crossings: Small, no problem.
Trail use: Very light.
Topographic Quadrangle: Huckleberry
Mountain.

It's never crowded at Brown's Meadow except maybe during hunting season. Trail Number 2a is a spur from the meadow that climbs to Wildcat Divide, a distance of about 2 miles. This spur is, naturally, used even less than Brown's Meadow.

Most of the trail leads through a deep north-facing forest, but Wildcat Divide is open country, frequently covered with flowers, and it offers a fine view. It's elk heaven—perhaps as close as we will come to ours as well.

Until 1976, this trail was just about dead due to lack of maintenance, but in that year the trail was re-cut, preventing hikers from wandering off on the numerous game trails. You still have to pay some attention, however.

This trail starts just south of Arizona Creek (across the creek from the junk cabin). Several parallel trails exist. They all go to the same place. Take one of these trails, keeping to the far west side of Brown's Meadow. Here you are near the rim of Arizona Creek's canyon, and there are also some views of the north part of the Tetons.

The trail crosses the meadow and then heads up toward a small densely-forested canyon. The canyon was cut by a tributary of Arizona Creek. The trail enters the forest. As it does so, you begin to climb. The climb is fairly steep for about a mile. You cross several small streams. Soon the forest begins to open up, and you walk through many beautiful flower-filled openings near the divide. From the first buttercups in early June amidst the snow-drifts to late August with its paintbrush, this trail is filled with flowers from here all the way to the divide.

The divide is broad and open. The scene is dominated by the impressive Wildcat Ridge just to the east. This long horizontal ridge with layered sandstone cliffs, bluish-green grass and flowery flanks is one of the most prominent features of the western Teton Wilderness.

To the west are the forest and open slopes of Kitten Ridge and to

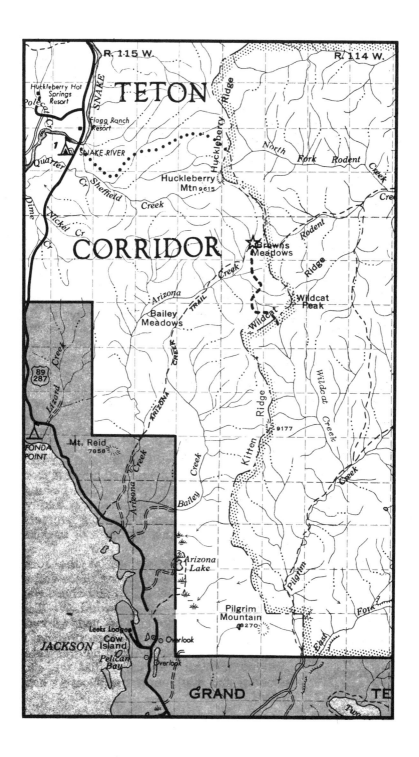

Across Wildcat Divide to Wildcat Ridge.

the south is a view down Wildcat Creek to Pilgrim Creek, and beyond that, Jackson Hole. The panorama is completed by the cliffs of Huckleberry Ridge to the north.

The Huckleberry Mountain U.S.G.S. topographic quadrangle shows a trail from the divide down Wildcat Creek (the creek isn't named on any map), ending at Trail Number 3 in Pilgrim Creek. This trail no longer exists, although parts of it can be found. Instead, the trip down Wildcat Creek is a beautiful, but rough, cross-country hike. Some maps also show a trail on top of Kitten Ridge to the west. No such trail exists, but the ridge is open on top and fairly level. It isn't a hard walk along it, and the views of the Tetons are tremendous.

24

View across Kitten Ridge to the Tetons from Wildcat Peak.

2b RODENT CREEK FROM BROWN'S MEADOW TO TRAIL 3c

Length: 5 miles.
Effort: 5 miles downstream, 6 ½ miles
   upstream.
Trail condition: Good to fair.
River crossings: Numerous, July 1.
Trail use: Very light.
Topographic Quadrangle: Huckleberry
   Mountain.

Since few people make it to Brown's Meadow, fewer still continue down Rodent Creek. This trail is very isolated. Until it was reworked in 1979, it was in poor condition. Now its condition is pretty good unless you go downstream below the point where Trails 3c and 3d depart.

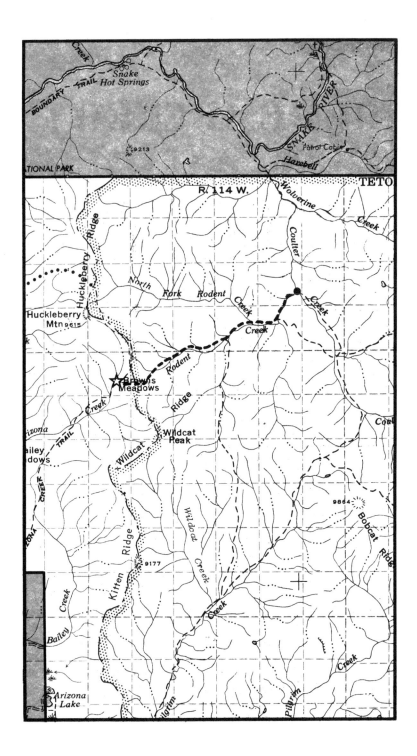

View across Rodent Creek from Wildcat Peak.

The trail starts at Brown's Meadow, either at the junk cabin or the grave. It goes on the level to the east end of the meadow, drops a bit through timber and crosses the headwaters of Rodent Creek which comes splashing down from Wildcat Ridge at the edge of another small meadow. From here the canyon deepens rapidly. The trail passes mostly through deep spruce-fir forest with a few openings, and it climbs at first 40, and then about 100 feet above the creek.

After about three miles, the trail drops to the creek and the little-used, but very scenic, East Rodent Creek Trail joins. The first major ford of Rodent Creek is here just below the confluence of East Rodent Creek, which tumbles down a steep canyon from Wildcat Ridge. The ford is probably safe after July 1. Hardly anyone gets into this country that early anyway.

From here for about a mile, the creek is crossed many times. The trail is confined to a small place next to the stream by the narrow canyon walls. Finally, after the confluence of primeval North Rodent Creek, a small meadow develops along the creek which continues to Trail 3d, the Wolverine Cut-off Trail. From here it is a short distance to Trail 3c, which is the end of the Rodent Creek Trail.

There are lots of good campsites on this trail. The creek is fair fishing for small cutthroat trout. Look for elk near Brown's Meadow.

3 PILGRIM CREEK

Length: 9½ miles.
Effort: 12½ miles.
Trail condition: Fair.
River crossings: Very many, July 15.
Trail use: Very light.
Topographic Quadrangles: Two Ocean
Lake, Huckleberry Mountain, Mt.
Hancock.

Pilgrim Creek is another good place to escape people, including wilderness travelers. The trail crosses the creek no fewer than 28 times! The stream is deep enough that you usually can't ford it until mid-July. A few other things function to detract use from this wild stream. First, the Pilgrim Creek Road leaves U.S. highway 89/287 (7.5 miles north of Moran Junction) at what is by mid-Summer a hot, beaten-out-looking flat. Here, after the Spring run-off is over, Pilgrim Creek is a trickle through the middle of a wide field of gravel. Third, the road to the trail starts out fair, but after a few miles it comes to a ford that requires a jeep. From this point you have to walk a half-mile to the trailhead. Worse, the vehicular traffic doesn't end at the trailhead, instead you follow a jeep track and motorcycle raceway for another ¾ mile or so. Finally, there are only very small fish in Pilgrim Creek.

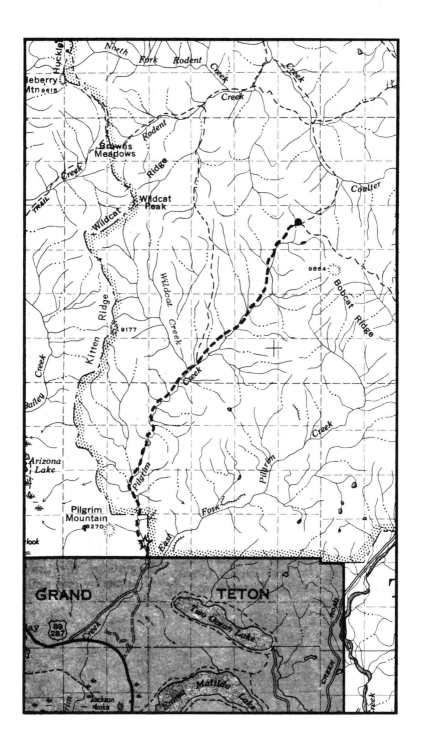

Down Pilgrim Creek to the Tetons.

Despite the poor introduction, Pilgrim Creek offers considerable variety, and it is an excellent wildlife area. It has an elk herd, numerous moose, deer, coyotes, even grizzly bear and three or four resident mountain lion. It is a heavily-forested canyon with many blue spruce and a large meadow in the middle of the canyon.

After the jeep trail dies, the pack trail wanders back and forth across the river through heavy spruce forest for about a mile. Look for moose here. Soon you walk past a burn of about 100 acres (dated from the Summer of 1977), and begin to climb out of the canyon. The canyon becomes a gorge cut in soft white rock, and the trail follows the east rim. Before long you descend into a rich, broad meadow that is almost two miles long. Numerous ponds provide a good view of waterfowl. This is also a good place to see moose and elk.

As you approach the top of the big meadow, you can see several faint trails leading into the forest on the left. These are the defunct Wildcat Creek Trail and the former beginning of the East Rodent Creek Trail (Number 3a), which now leaves the trail you're on about a half mile further up Pilgrim Creek. By the way, the Two Ocean Lake topographic quadrangle is wrong. It shows both the Wildcat Creek and the East Rodent Creek Trail leaving at the top of the meadow.

On the Pilgrim Creek trail.

Meadow in the middle reaches of Pilgrim Creek.

The trail re-enters the forest and soon crosses a small, slow, clear stream with a deep mud bottom. About 25 yards up from this crossing, the stream emerges from a spring—good-tasting water. Before long Wildcat Creek is crossed just above its junction with Pilgrim Creek. At approximately this point, you can begin to see the Tetons if you look back down Pilgrim Creek. Their sharp crests rise above the gentle, forested ridges that line Pilgrim Creek.

A short distance past Wildcat Creek the present-day junction with East Rodent Creek trail is reached. It leaves in a dense stand of lodgepole pine to the left. There is a sign. At about this point the trail begins to climb. You cross the creek for the umpteenth time and soon Pilgrim Creek is nearly a hundred feet below in a small gorge. The creek rises to meet you. Cross the creek again, and then climb in earnest. Pilgrim Creek is 400 feet below in a forested canyon. Small openings on the trail give a good view of Bobcat Ridge to the east. Descend to the creek and then climb through open slopes and spruce-fir timber with several more crossings of small, splashing Pilgrim Creek to the divide. Here is a junction of four trails. Straight on, the trail (3b) leads to rarely-visited Coulter Creek. To the left is the obscure Wildcat Ridge Trail. I tried following this trail here and also at its other end (Wildcat Divide), but soon lost all traces of it. The trail on the right is the West Cutoff Trail (5), a lovely and lonesome hike.

3a EAST RODENT CREEK

Length: 6 miles.
Effort: 9 miles from Pilgrim Creek to Rodent
Creek; 8 miles from Rodent Creek to
Pilgrim Creek.
Trail condition: Fair.
River crossings: Numerous, small in East
Rodent Creek.
Trail use: Very light.
Topographic Quadrangles: Two Ocean
Lake, Huckleberry Mountain.

This trail offers excellent views of the Pilgrim Creek country as it climbs out of Pilgrim Creek. It ascends to a low spot on Wildcat Ridge, passing through forest and open slopes. If you want to see or hunt elk, this trail is a good bet.

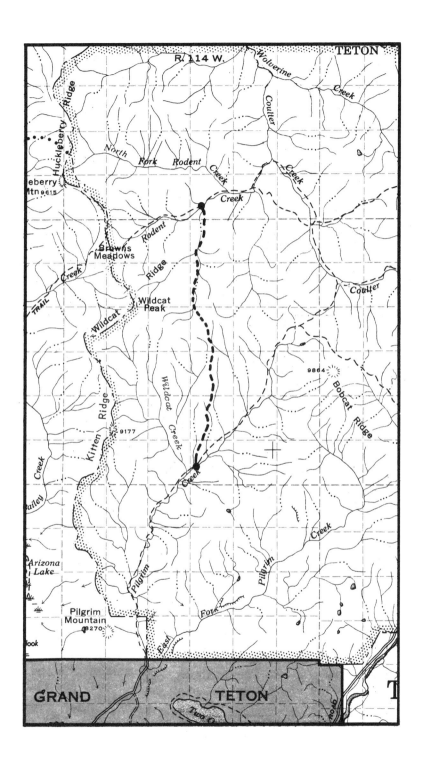

The East Rodent Creek Trail connects Pilgrim Creek with Rodent Creek. Both of these trails are seldom traveled. Thus, the East Rodent Creek Trail receives still less use.

The climb on the Rodent Creek side of Wildcat Ridge isn't quite as great as the Pilgrim Creek side. It is also a bit steeper. I describe it here from Pilgrim Creek (Trail Number 3).

Our trail leaves the Pilgrim Creek Trail at a signed junction about a quarter mile upstream, past the point where Pilgrim and Wildcat creek join. The trail obviously is not used much as you look at its narrow tread, but it is easily visible as it heads gradually upward through a thick stand of bare-trunked lodgepole pine.

Soon it begins to climb more steeply and crosses through small meadows as well as the forest. About a third of the way up the ridge, you enter a large open area (beautiful flowers from early to mid-Summer). Here the tread becomes somewhat difficult to follow for about 1 ½ miles. You'll work up a good sweat, with the climb continuous and on a southward-facing slope, but it's a sublime view down Pilgrim Creek. You see Pilgrim Creek's gentle and densely-forested slopes, Bobcat Ridge to the left, and the big meadow in the middle of Pilgrim Creek. The Tetons rise in the distance.

Clearing near the junction of trails 3, 3b, and 5.

The trail continues upward through open slopes and patches of forest. The gently sloping summit is attained at the edge of a meadow. Here the old Wildcat Ridge Trail crosses. I haven't described this trail, due to its lack of use and difficulty finding its two ends. Parts of the trail are distinct, however. As a cross country hike, a walk along the top of Wildcat Ridge provides a terrific view.

Beyond the summit, the trail drops abruptly into East Rodent Creek—a steep, narrow and damp, northward facing canyon. Here, amidst heavy spruce and fir forest and steep slopes all around, you sense that you are in an immense wilderness.

The trail is wet late into the Summer in this canyon. You cross East Rodent Creek (not named on the maps) several times, but these are not difficult crossings except during maximum run-off. You're unlikely to be in the area at that time of the year anyway. The trail ends just after fording Rodent Creek (July 1), where it joins Trail Number 2b.

3b COULTER CREEK—RODENT CREEK CUT-OFF

Length: 6½ miles.
Effort: 7½ miles from the top of Pilgrim
     Creek to junction with Trail Number 3d;
     9 miles in the opposite direction.
Trail condition: Poor to very poor.
River crossings: Numerous, July 20.
Trail use: Very light.
Topographic Quadrangle: Mt. Hancock.

This trail is probably the least-used of those described in this book. It leads into very remote, heavily-forested country. There is a requirement of at least two hard days' travel to get into this area from any trailhead.

The trail is poorly-maintained and in places the Forest Service maps and the Mt. Hancock U.S.G.S. quadrangle are incorrect regarding the trail's location. If you run into anyone else on this trail, it will be a miracle.

The trail begins on a scenic semi-open divide at the head of Pilgrim Creek. Here, there is a four-way trail junction at a tall pole. A

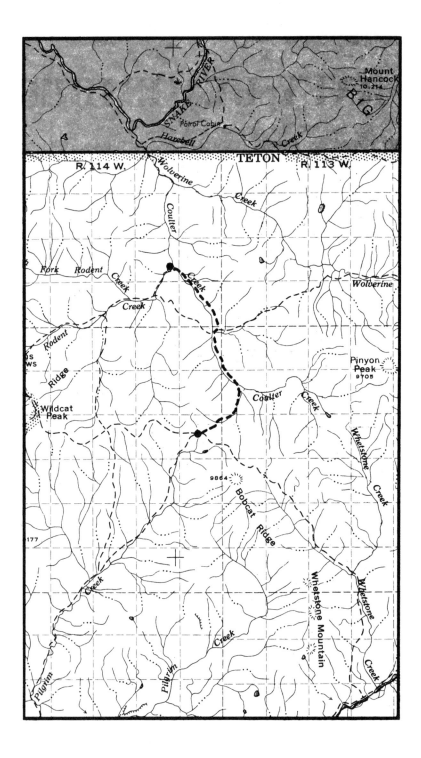

sign tacked to the pole points to the trail leading across the divide and reads "Coulter Creek." The track is obvious enough at its start. It passes a small pond with flowers all around in mid-Summer, and then it begins to descend quickly. In about a mile-and-a-half, the trail drops 600 feet as it follows down a small tributary of Coulter Creek. You come to a meadow at the lower end of this tributary canyon. In the meadow you will lose the trail. Walk through the meadow, trying to keep your feet dry, to Coulter Creek. Coulter Creek is a nice stream here with many medium size, round rocks in its bed.

At this point, all the maps show a trail coming down Coulter Creek to join the one you are on (or just lost). The maps are wrong. This trail was long ago obliterated by lack of use and the multitudinous earth-flows in upper Coulter Creek. You can make a cross country hike upstream if you want. The first mile-and-a-half is hard. The creek flows through a narrow forested canyon. Above it, however, is a large peaceful meadow where you get a view of 9705-foot Pinyon Peak.

Coulter Creek does have a trail (of sorts) below the confluence of the tributary. It took us two hours to find it, but our misfortune led to this description which may save you from the same predicament. Just below the confluence meadow, Coulter Creek runs through a short canyon. Pick your way about ¼ mile down this canyon, then cross to the right side of the creek. Angle slowly up and away from the creek, and you should hit the trail. If you miss it, keep going downstream. Eventually you'll find it.

The canyon broadens a bit and the trail crosses Coulter Creek several times. There are many good campsites. Crossing the creek isn't easy until about the end of July on most years, although in the drought year of 1977 we crossed it in late June. There are many grassy meadows (often swampy) along the creek. Each time the trail passes through one you will probably lose it unless you watch carefully for the blazes on the older trees. After about two miles, you come to the remains of a very small cabin. Off to the left across the river, an eagle-eyed person can see a blaze. This is the Rodent/Wolverine Creek Trail (Number 3c). It, and the Coulter Creek Trail, are one and the same for about 1/8 mile downstream from the cabin. Just below the cabin you cross a major tributary of Coulter Creek (sometimes called "Middle Creek"). Here, climb briefly and come to a sign. Trail 3c leads to the right into Wolverine Creek. The sign tells you that the faint track straight ahead is the Rodent Creek Cut-off, although the maps call it the Coulter Creek Trail. While Trail 3c to the right is faint, the trail ahead is really faint.

Forge ahead following the very faint trail. It soon comes to a small meadow and turns to the right for a short distance. You may lose the trail here unless you note that it soon turns back to the left

Seldom-visited Coulter Creek.

and continues down Coulter Creek. It is absolutely crucial that you look for blazes from here on.

Below this point, Coulter Creek runs into a steep, often vertical-walled gorge. The Coulter Creek Trail follows high above the river on a bench covered with lodgepole pine. The trail, though hardly-ever used, isn't too hard to follow in this timber as long as you look for blazes. As the trail begins to descend into Coulter Creek, however, it becomes very hard to find and the deadfall makes travel slow. You can find the trail, if you are careful. If you aren't careful, you may get lost—not a good idea in this densely-forested and somewhat feature-less portion of the Wilderness.

The trail comes down to Coulter Creek about 200 yards above where Rodent Creek tumbles in. A narrow meadow abuts the creek here. Part of it is mushy, but there are some nice campsites here, the only ones in the general area.

The faint trail crosses right at the Coulter Creek/Rodent Creek junction. This isn't an easy ford (about late July). It is best to cross Coulter Creek and then Rodent Creek. If both look too hard, try about 75 yards downstream. A conspicuous blaze on the right side of Rodent Creek marks the location of the trail's continuation. Unfortu-nately, the tread soon fades and blazes all but disappear. If you do find the trail, disappointment soon follows. In the 40 or 50 years since the trail was maintained, Rodent Creek has washed large parts away. The easiest thing to do is just hike up Rodent Creek (cross-country) for about 1½ miles. Finally, you come to a sign that says Rodent/Wolverine Trail (Number 3c), and here our trail ends. If you follow the now-easily-visible trail a few yards further up Rodent Creek, you come to the so-called "Wolverine Cut-off" Trail (3d) which leaves at a sharp angle to the right at a sign. Unfortunately from the standpoint of clarity, the maps call this trail (3d) the Coulter Creek Trail, but the sign says "Wolverine Cut-off." I've accepted the sign for the purposes of this book.

In sum, Trail 3b offers you a fine wilderness experience and allows you to use your route-finding skills. I would like to add that below its junction with Rodent Creek, Coulter Creek runs through a beautiful primeval canyon. You can hike down this in tennis shoes (a must as the creek often fills the canyon from bank-to-bank). Take a fishing pole and catch some of many small Snake River Cutthroat Trout. Hardly anyone does this. You can probably count on the fingers of one hand the people who have walked all the way down Coulter Creek Canyon to Wolverine Creek.

3c RODENT-WOLVERINE

Length: 5½ miles.
Effort: 7 miles from Rodent Creek to
Wolverine Creek; 7¼ miles the oppo-
site direction.
Trail condition: Poor.
River crossings: Two, July 20.
Trail use: Very light.
Topographic Quadrangles: Huckleberry
Mountain, Mt. Hancock.

This obscure trail leads from Rodent Creek across rarely-visited Coulter Creek and then into remote Wolverine Creek. The trip is mostly through dense forest and subdued topography.

The trail starts at a sign just a short distance down Rodent Creek from where Trail Number 3d (the Wolverine Cut-off) leaves the Rodent Creek Trail. The Huckleberry Mountain U.S.G.S. quadrangle incorrectly shows our trail (which could be thought as a continuation

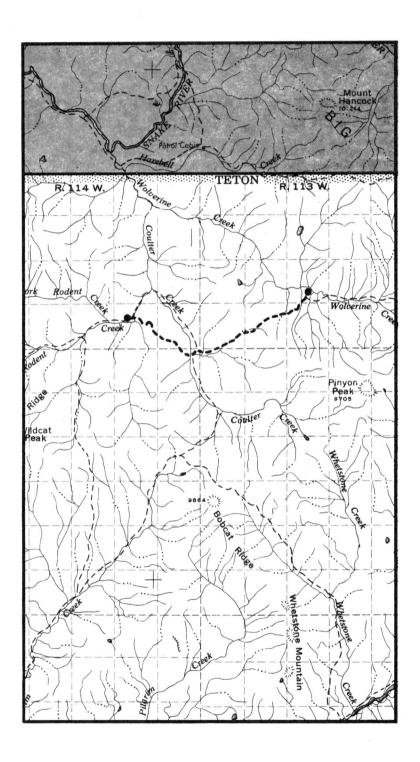

of the Rodent Creek Trail, Number 2b) leaving Rodent Creek before Trail 3d rather than after.

The Rodent-Wolverine Trail immediately fords Rodent Creek and climbs about 400 feet through continuous forest over a broad ridge and down into Coulter Creek in about two miles. This two miles is pretty uneventful, unless you get lost! Ford Coulter Creek (possible about July 20), and find the faint Coulter Creek Trail (3b) on the other side. Follow this trail for about 1/8 of a mile to the ford of a tributary of Coulter Creek. This is Middle Creek. Just beyond this ford a sign is encountered which, at last look, showed the Rodent Creek Cut-off Trail straight ahead and the trail you want to the right.

From the sign the trail climbs about 300 feet through forest and small meadows until it comes to a long and mushy meadow from which Middle Creek emerges. Beaver ponding will probably cause you to lose the faint track of the trail here, but you can route find by heading for a low spot in the ridge ahead. From here, on the trail, or cross country, you can't help but descend about 600 feet through forest to a big meadow through which flows little-known Wolverine Creek.

3d WOLVERINE CUT-OFF

Length: 4 miles.
Effort: 4½ miles from Rodent Creek to Yellowstone Park; 5 miles the opposite direction.
Trail condition: Fair, deteriorating to very poor.
River crossings: Two, August 1.
Trail use: Very low.
Topographic Quadrangles: Huckleberry Mountain, Mt. Hancock.

This is an interesting and really "way back" trail that is shown in the wrong place on all of the maps. Its north end is hard to find, but it's not too hard to get to Yellowstone from Rodent Creek. However, you'll probably get lost if you try to follow it northward from Yellowstone National Park.

The trail starts in a meadow along Rodent Creek where a sign announces "Wolverine Cut-off." The maps all label this trail "Coulter Creek Trail," but I'll go with the sign since nothing else the maps say about this trail is correct. The same maps also show this trail as leaving Rodent Creek further downstream than it actually does and below the exit of Trail Number 3c. This isn't so, or at least it hasn't been so for years. The Rodent-Wolverine Trail (Number 3c) leaves Rodent Creek about a hundred yards down from our trail.

The Wolverine Cut-off climbs quickly through a patch of forest, and then it goes steeply up an open slope covered with tall flowers and forbs and heads into the forest. For a short distance into the forest, you can see through the trees the lovely, green riparian meadow along Rodent Creek and the thick, wild forest to its south, where travels the unseen Rodent-Wolverine Trail (Number 3c).

Walk through the forest for perhaps 1 ½ miles, then you come to a steep place on the trail. Climb up this short steep pitch of the trail. On top, you stand in the open on top of a conglomerate cliff. The rock pushes away the forest for a grand view. Far below courses Coulter Creek through a possibly never traversed gorge. Not far on the other side rises massive Big Game Ridge, home of many elk. This is the best view of Big Game Ridge anywhere in the Teton Wilderness (or Yellowstone Park). Everywhere the land is covered with dense forest. In fact, this area has the largest expanse of unbroken forest in the Teton Wilderness. There is irony to this. In the late 1800s, this area was reported as a large burn, similar to the Mink Creek burn of today. The Mink Creek area, about thirteen linear miles to the east, was then unburned—a vast forest. The wilderness is always changing.

The trail to the rock viewpoint isn't bad, but just beyond it the trail splits into many parallel trails kept up by game. The maps show the trail descending into Coulter Creek, crossing it at the end of its gorge and going up Wolverine Creek. However, the trail in lower Wolverine Creek is just about dead, and there is no signed (or obvious unsigned) turn-off from these game trails to Wolverine Creek. Be smart and just keep going northward through the deep, dense forest on one of the game trails. Doing this, you can't help but come to a creek about half the size of Rodent Creek which has its source on the northern end of Huckleberry Ridge.

Ford this stream, and on the other side you're in Yellowstone National Park. You'll probably find a boundary marker.

Follow this stream down a short distance to where it flows into Wolverine Creek. Here the forest opens and there are places to camp. You can't camp in Yellowstone without a backcountry permit.

A trail crosses Wolverine Creek here, but you don't have to make the ford if it looks too tough (which it well may be) unless you want to follow the South Boundary Trail over Big Game Ridge (Trail Number 7d). Wolverine Creek is 2-3 feet deep, wide, has a moderate current, and is filled with round, slippery rocks. If you want to go down the

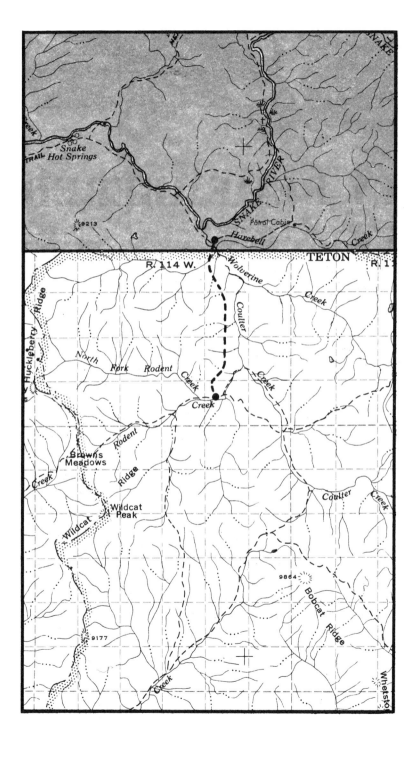

Snake River and into Yellowstone, you can walk cross country a short distance and rejoin it because the trail quickly recrosses Wolverine Creek anyway.

The country quickly opens up into a lush, open stream valley as you move north into Yellowstone. Near where Wolverine Creek and the Snake River blend their waters, there are fine campsites everywhere. Don't camp in Yellowstone unless you have one of their backcountry permits, however, and don't bring a dog. The Park Service is death on dogs. They say dogs harm the environment (unlike the snowmobiles that roar over Yellowstone's landscape in the Winter with full Park Service approval). A Park Ranger from Harebell cabin comes down to check for violators from time-to-time.

Wolverine Creek is sometimes about the same size as the Snake River where they join. One Summer we caught a party heading up Wolverine Creek, thinking it was the Snake River. The Snake River is the stream to the left for those of you coming upstream on the Snake River trail. All the streams here are good fishing for cutthroat trout and whitefish.

4 ATLANTIC-PACIFIC CREEK

Length: 30 miles.
Effort: 33 miles from Pacific Creek trail
   head to Yellowstone Meadows.
Trail condition: Good.
River crossings: Six, July 30.
Trail use: Heavy.
Topographic Quadrangles: Whetstone
   Mountain, Gravel Mountain, Mt.
   Hancock, Two Ocean Pass.

The Pacific and Atlantic Creek Trail is one of the major arteries of the Wilderness. It is a long trail, leading past a variety of wilderness scenes and into the heart of the Upper Yellowstone River country. The trail is in good condition, but it is a bit crowded in spots. I've listed its use as heavy (two or more parties a day), but use is quite a bit more than this in lower Pacific Creek and near its end at Yellowstone Meadows. Upper Pacific Creek isn't really very busy. Maybe two or three parties pass by a day, but they usually don't stay to camp. They're on their way somewhere else.

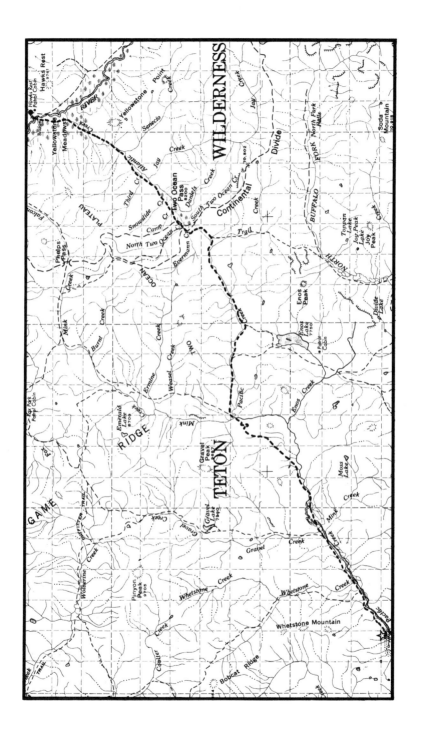

In the middle reaches of Pacific Creek.

You should note that the lower part of Pacific Creek also gets a lot of use by cattle every year for a month, beginning about mid-July. Some Wilderness visitors object to cattle. At this time of year, they should seek another trail.

The Pacific Creek Road leaves U.S. 89/287, 1.2 miles north of Moran Junction. There is an entrance station for Grand Teton National Park on the highway just north of Moran Junction, but you won't have to pay the $2.00 entrance fee if you tell them you are heading up Pacific Creek to backpack in the national forest.

The Pacific Creek Road is easy to spot. It is paved, and leaves the highway on the right. There is a sign. About 1½ miles from the highway, the Two Ocean Lake Road leaves to the left. Just past this point you come to another junction. Take the unpaved fork to the left. A sign should tell you that this is the road to the Teton Wilderness. From here it is several miles to the trailhead, which is exactly at the edge of the Wilderness. There is space to park a lot of cars.

This is the second busiest Teton Wilderness trailhead. There may be a lot of backpackers, pack strings and day hikers here. If you're willing to take the first side trail (Number 5), you only have to tolerate crowds for about 1½ miles.

The trail climbs a bench along Pacific Creek and heads into lodgepole pine. Be sure to sign-in at the trail register. The count of the large number of people who use the Wilderness helps to preserve and create new units of the Wilderness System.

The problem is this. Many politicians believe the old yarn perpetuated by the timber industry about how only the "hardy" few ever visit any part of a forest where there isn't a road. Therefore, they argue roadless lands should be opened up for the benefit of the motorcycle, jeep, and assorted land-ripping paraphernalia, upon which rides what they like to call the "average American." Meanwhile, of course, their "public-spirited" efforts on behalf of the average person gets them a timber haul road built.

You follow a broad trail (actually an old road) for about two miles through forest. There are occasional views of Pacific Creek—a nice-sized stream that is good fishing for cutthroat trout and too many whitefish. If you walk down to the stream, you will find places to camp.

At about a mile, pass by a cabin which is down in the forest by the river. Next cross a small stream just at the head of a big bend in Pacific Creek. Immediately past this creek is a sign that says "Gravel Creek 5, Two Ocean Pass 19, Trailhead 2." Actually, Gravel Creek is only 2 or 3 miles away and the trailhead is about 1½ miles. I mention this spot because the Whetstone Trail (Number 5) leaves obscurely here to the left. The first time I came up Pacific Creek I couldn't find the Whetstone Trail. The trouble is, trail Number 5 has a sign, but it is hidden about ten yards up-trail from its beginning. It's easy to miss. **If you cross a second small creek, you have gone too far.**

Soon after crossing the second small creek, you come to Whetstone Creek, running down a narrow channel in the middle of a delta of gravel. Most years you can ford it by June 20. The rock in the stream has a texture similar to whetstone used to sharpen knives.

Soon you enter a huge meadow which is 4 or 5 miles long and about a mile wide. Surrounding the meadow are low, forested mountains. The meadow is covered with low-growing willows, grass, and flowers. About ½ mile into the meadow, you get a splendid view of the Tetons if you turn around. A medium telephoto lens is necessary for the best picture—the Grand Teton rising above the flowers and forest.

I've never seen wildlife in the big meadow in the five times I've been through, but then I've never camped there, and it would be an excellent place to stay. Campsites are unlimited. The only trouble is some years there are livestock and the meadow looks kind of beaten out then.

As you strike out for Gravel Creek, the numerous paths across the meadow give mute testimony to the heavy use the trail receives. Sometimes the trail consists of as many as ten parallel tracks cut into the meadow sod.

Gravel Creek lives up to its name, running through a sparsely-vegetated and rocky part of the meadow. You can ford this cobble-bottomed creek about the end of June. On the other side you briefly cross over a rocky bench and then drop back down into the big meadow. Before long you come to a major ford of Pacific Creek. The stream is slow here, but deep. August 1 is the usual time that you can make it. This need not spoil an earlier trip, however. Just walk to the extreme left side of the meadow (the northern side). Walk here cross country or on an outfitter trail all the way to the top of the meadow where the main trail joins.

The main trail keeps to the middle of the meadow and crosses Pacific Creek once again at a wide crossing near the head of the big meadow. The character of the trip changes abruptly as you enter lodgepole forest and the valley narrows to a canyon.

In a small meadow in the forest a sign marks the junction with the Enos Creek Outfitter Trail (Number 9a). From this point on, the USGS Gravel Mountain quadrangle does not show the Pacific Creek Trail, only Trail 9a. This is an error. The main trail climbs about 650 feet in 1½ miles, following a small tributary of Pacific Creek over a shoulder of Gravel Peak. Trail 9a is definitely not the way to go unless your destination is Enos Lake. It also involves a very difficult ford of Pacific Creek.

After the climb, the trail descends abruptly almost 600 feet to the Mink Creek crossing. There is a place to camp here. Mink Creek is a beautiful, and quite large creek. It rolls out of an impassable gorge right at its confluence with Pacific Creek. This too is a hard ford until about July 20. The creek is large and a little swift with many slippery and various-sized rocks in its bed. One time, about August 10, I talked to some people who did the ford in their bare feet. Their story made me wince. You should bring tennis shoes for these crossings.

The trail climbs very steeply about 200 feet out of the canyon. You pass the Mink Creek Trail (Number 7) in the process, and emerge in a big meadow on a bench way above Pacific Creek. There are some fine views from this vicinity of the canyon that confines Pacific Creek.

In about a mile, at the head of this meadow a spur to the Mink Creek Trail leaves. Go from here past a small pond and through forest and meadow to another ford of Pacific Creek (not very hard). Soon you come to the junction with Trail 9b and then 9c, both leading to the beautiful north end of Enos Lake. Near these junctions, terraced volcanic cliffs of the Two Ocean Plateau loom to your left. You have left the Pinyon Peak Highlands with their sedimentary rocks and are now in the Absarokas.

The expansive Pacific Creek Meadows at the junction of the Gravel Creek trail.

The meadows and patches of forest become increasingly lovely for the next four or five miles as you follow diminishing Pacific Creek to famous Two Ocean Pass.

Two Ocean Pass is the Continental Divide, but it doesn't look at all like a pass. Instead it is a broad wet meadow with an almost imperceptible slope. Uniquely it drains into both oceans. Even more dramatic drainage anomalies occur just to the north and south. If you take Trail 4a, which leaves to the left on top of the pass, you'll soon come to "Parting of the Waters." North Two Ocean Creek tumbles down from its source on the Two Ocean Plateau and splits into two streams at the base of a large tree. One branch becomes Atlantic Creek and one Pacific Creek. A trout can actually swim over the Continental Divide here. A sign reads "Atlantic Ocean 3488 mi., Pacific Ocean 1353 mi."

If you walk back across the meadow, to the base of the Buffalo Plateau which forms the valley wall to the south (it seems odd to call a pass a valley, but that's the way it seems), you'll come to another parting. South Two Ocean Creek splits as well, although the parting is not quite as dramatic. Some think that this was discovered first, however. Today it is little-known, by-passed by hundreds of travelers.

The trail down Atlantic Creek is easy. The creek meanders nearby, full of fish. The ford at the bottom of the canyon is substantial. Finally, you emerge into a large valley, the valley of the Upper Yellowstone—almost twenty miles long and a mile or more wide.

Here at Yellowstone Meadows, as it's called, you are at least 25 linear miles from any road—the farthest such point in the lower 48 states. It's too bad that that's as far as you can get away, but were it not for the Wilderness Act you'd probably be standing on a highway today (or "motor nature trail" as such roads are euphemistically called).

Despite its remoteness, Yellowstone Meadows gets lots of foot and horse traffic. The Yellowstone River, which you soon cross on a bridge, is overflowing with big cutthroat trout. Many, many parties come in to fish each Summer.

Though people are abundant, so is game. Many moose roam this valley. It's perfect habitat with its willows, patches of forest, sloughs, and flowered meadowland. The area has lots of bears too. Clean those fish away from camp.

The trail ends ½ mile across the river at the Hawk's Rest Patrol Cabin (usually occupied by a wilderness ranger). A half mile north of the cabin is Bridger Lake, just off of the Yellowstone River. This jewel is full of large trout and is the summer home most years for two trumpeter swans. There are campsites by the lake. Here you see the reflected image of the massive Trident to the north or Hawks Rest Mountain to the south. This is a serene place, disturbed only by wilderness fishermen or moose swimming in the lake's waters.

4a TWO OCEAN PLATEAU

Length: 6 miles.
Effort: 9½ miles from Two Ocean Pass; 8½
miles from Mink Creek to Two Ocean
Pass.
Trail condition: Fair.
River crossings: Small streams.
Trail use: Light.
Topographic Quadrangle: Two Ocean Pass.

This trail takes you on a steep climb to the top of the world—well, anyway to the top of the Two Ocean Plateau which seems like the top of the world. On top is a fine view of the Tetons, a riot of wildflowers in the tundra about the end of July, and a good chance to see elk.

Most begin this climb at Two Ocean Pass (see the description of Trail 4). The trail leaves the meadow, passes through some timber to the unique parting of the waters, crosses north Two Ocean Creek, and climbs steeply about 800 feet through forest and open slopes that provide a beautiful view of Two Ocean Pass below and the wall of the Buffalo Plateau to the south. Next the trail levels out for about ½ mile until it crosses north Two Ocean Creek again. The hiker now climbs another 100 feet through increasingly alpine country to the broad plateau top. The trail leads amid flowers past several ponds that beckon you to sit and bask in the intense sunshine (but if dark clouds are gathering, you should get off the top as fast as you can). The middle of three ponds has a small stream emerging. This is the source of Burnt Creek. This pond makes a nice foreground for a photo of the distant, yet dramatic Tetons.

The top of the plateau is an easy and beautiful cross country hike. It rises slightly as you head along it toward the northeast, culminating at Two Ocean Point, elevation 10,216 feet, at the very end of the plateau. Here you peer over an abrupt drop-off for a panoramic view of Yellowstone Meadows, Hawks Rest Mountain, the claw-like Trident in Yellowstone, and the high Thorofare Plateau to the east and southeast. The walk to this rewarding view is about four miles off the trail. If you do it, expect to see elk (maybe in large numbers).

The trail descends into Mink Creek at a good rate, though less so than on the Two Ocean Pass side of the plateau. It is through forest and open country. To the north, across the headwaters of Mink Creek at Phelps Pass, stretches the continuation of the Two Ocean Plateau, green except where flower fields show other colors, with patches of

51

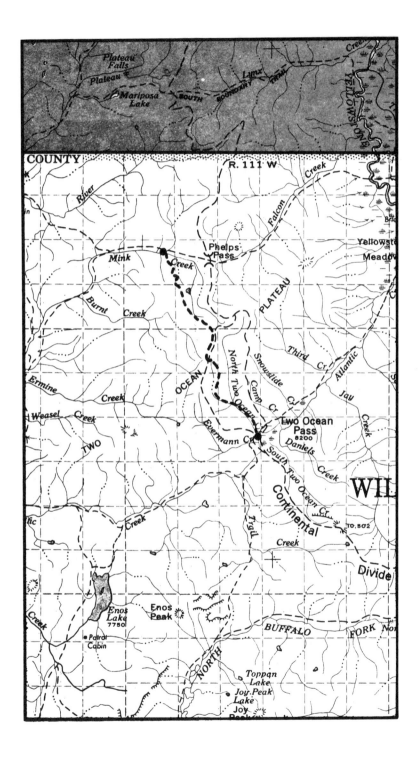

spruce timber. The trail crosses the two small creeks that join to create Mink Creek and meets the Mink Creek trail about a mile west of Phelps Pass.

5 WHETSTONE CREEK-WEST CUT-OFF

Length: 9 miles.
Effort: 13½ miles from Pacific Creek to the head of Pilgrim Creek via the west fork of Whetstone Creek; 9½ miles the opposite direction.
Trail condition: Fair.
River crossings: Three, June 20.
Trail use: Very light.
Topographic Quadrangles: Whetstone Mountain, Mt. Hancock.

This is another typically little-used trail of the western Teton Wilderness. It starts from the heavily used Pacific Creek Trail (Trail 4), crosses a shoulder of Whetstone Mountain, descends to Whetstone Creek, and follows the west fork of Whetstone Creek canyon over the northern end of Bobcat Ridge to the remote country between Pilgrim Creek and Coulter Creek.

Look carefully for the start of Trail Number 5. It lies between two small creeks at the head of a big bend in Pacific Creek about 1½ miles from the start of the Pacific Creek Trail. There is no trail sign marking the trail, but it takes off near the spot where a sign on the Pacific Creek trail says, "Gravel Creek 5, Two Ocean Pass 19, Trailhead 2." And once on the faint path that is Trail Number 5 there is a sign that says, "Whetstone Creek 3, Coulter Creek 8." Actually, it is more like eleven miles to Coulter Creek.

The first three miles to the crossing of Whetstone Creek are really scenic. The trail goes through pine, spruce, and fir with many open meadows and past a number of beautiful ponds as it climbs about 800 feet over a shoulder of Whetstone Mountain. Near the top of the climb you earn views to the east of the gentle forested ridges that dominate the land around Pacific Creek. The last time I was here in June 1977 great clouds of pollen were being lifted from the lodgepole pine with the wind. The passing of these golden mists created a heavenly effect.

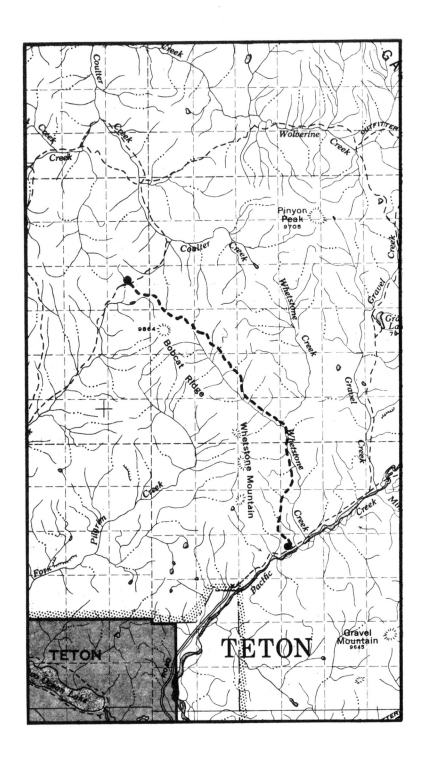

View down Pilgrim Creek from Bobcat Ridge.

The trail descends slightly to the base of Whetstone Mountain with its cliffs towering overhead. Here is a good spot for lunch in the streamside meadows.

Whetstone Creek is crossed twice in quick succession at about three miles. There are some small fish in the creek. You will notice a narrow canyon entering from the right (NE). This is actually the main fork of Whetstone Creek, and all the maps show a trail going up it. Unfortunately for the loop-trip planner, this trail has expired. Lack of maintenance, lack of use, and numerous earth movements have obliterated it.

The trail heads up the left fork and crosses the stream to its right side. The maps call this the West Cut-off Trail. Across the stream now, you head through a small wet meadow. Be careful to accurately locate the trail on the other side where it enters deep forest and then climbs steeply about 200 feet in elevation.

Next, the trail climbs steadily, but not steeply, for about four miles. All the while the trail parallels the stream which lies about a quarter mile to the left, down 200 feet, and out of sight.

The trail-side scenery becomes increasingly dominated by meadows as you climb. As a bonus there are quite a few ponds near

Whetstone Mountain from Whetstone Creek.

the trail. Beside the ponds, or on the many small tributary streams, are many fine camping spots. All of the country between the two forks of Whetstone Creek is loaded with ponds. These are the product of the unstable geology of the area. The Cretaceous sediments that comprise these soft, but steep ridges, begin to slide when they are wet. These earthflows, or "slumps" as they are often called, have created a hummocky landscape over thousands of years that catches melt water in its many small depressions.

The trail becomes increasingly faint as you approach the top of the west fork of Whetstone Creek. The meadows and the slumps make the tread hard to find. Watch for blazes on the trees. Along the climb to the summit are good views of 9800 foot high Bobcat Ridge with its steep cliffs breaking up green, meadowy flanks. Actually Bobcat Ridge is but an extension of Whetstone Mountain. They are the same geologic formation, the two being separated only by a pass. On the west side of Bobcat Ridge lies the rarely seen country in the trailless East Fork of Pilgrim Creek. You might want to go there some time when you want to be really lonesome.

Just below the summit the trail disappears completely, but the divide is easy to find. Here, standing alone amid the flowers, is a pole to mark the trail.

Past this summit meadow, the tread is easy to find. It enters timber and so the tread is better. In addition, it was recut in 1976. The trail is a bit mushy though. You squeesh, squeesh through the damp earth while water-loving globeflowers line the trail. Along this part you also get a glimpse of Big Game Ridge in its entirety. There aren't many trailside views of this massive ridge.

Soon the trail drops very steeply about 400 feet to the divide between Pilgrim Creek and Coulter Creek. The trail ends near a pond on the divide. Here a pole marks the trail junction—Pilgrim Creek on the left, Coulter Creek to the right, and the near-defunct Wildcat Ridge trail straight ahead. There are a lot of level spots here to camp, but little water. If you drop down slightly into Pilgrim Creek, you will find room on the edge of a meadow for two or three tents near the start of splashing Pilgrim Creek.

6 GRAVEL CREEK

Length: 7 miles.
Effort: 9½ miles.
Trail condition: Fair.
River crossings: Three, July 10.
Trail use: Medium.
Topographic Quadrangles: Whetstone
Mountain, Gravel Mountain, Mt.
Hancock.

This trail gets more use than most of the trails in the western half of the Wilderness, but a lot of the traffic goes to Gravel Lake. You don't encounter many folks north of there. The country in Gravel Creek is similar to that of Whetstone Creek, but Gravel Creek is perhaps twice the size. You cross it three times. Parts are good fishing, yet most of the creek is rarely fished because the trail keeps a good distance from the creek, especially in the stream's middle reaches where it runs through a scenic gorge. I think the forest service would do well to build the trail closer to the creek. It would greatly improve the trailside scenery.

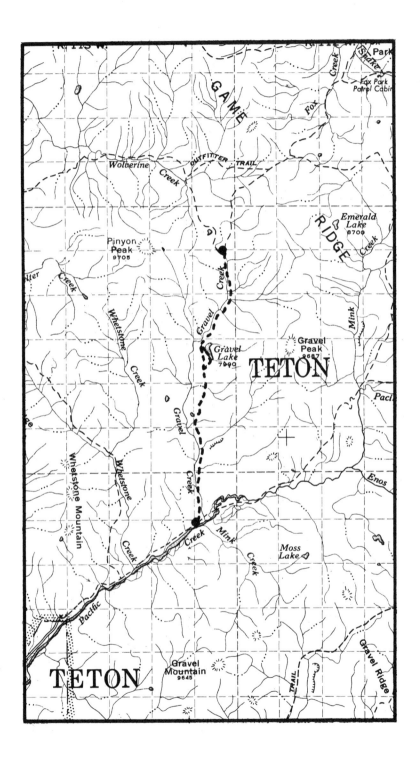

It's easy to locate the trailhead. You leave the Pacific Creek Trail (Number 4) in the broad Pacific Creek Meadow. You can see a pole with a sign marking the trailhead at least a mile away when you are coming up Pacific Creek.

Once on the trail, you climb a rocky bench which is perhaps twenty feet above the level of Pacific Creek Meadow and head northward through a patch of lodgepole pine to a crossing where the stream runs through several channels amid much river gravel. Another crossing is reached in a quarter-mile. Here Gravel Creek is deeper and swifter. The final crossing comes with a walk of yet another quarter-mile. Now the trail climbs abruptly up an open sidehill and then passes into the forest, leaving the creek for two miles— almost until you reach Gravel Lake. There are lots of ups and downs on this forested part of the trail, and there are few views. You do pass near several attractive ponds, however.

Finally, you approach and pass under a cliff. Behind this lies Gravel Lake. The trail drops down almost to Gravel Creek. You cross a stream that flows into Gravel Creek. This is the outlet of Gravel Lake. Shortly thereafter you come to the spur trail to Gravel Lake. It's about a quarter mile and an easy climb to the lake.

Gravel Lake is 1/3 mile long and perhaps 1/8 mile wide. It offers good fishing. Completely surrounded by forest, campsites for a large number of people are limited.

Back on the main trail beyond the lake, Gravel Creek is followed more closely than before. The walk is now scenic with numerous open places that give you a view of the steep slopes of Pinyon Peak. Around the openings stand the tall spires of the spruce and fir forest. Camping here is very good.

As you march deeper into the wilderness you begin to climb and cross the headwater tributaries of Gravel Creek. After ascending about 400 feet, you come to a meadow where the trail divides.

6a   BIG GAME RIDGE CUT-OFF

Length: 3 miles.
Effort: 4 miles from the end of the Gravel
*   Creek Trail to the Snake River Trail; 3*
*   miles the opposite direction.*
Trail condition: Fair.
River crossings: None of importance.
Trail use: Light.
Topographic Quadrangle: Mt. Hancock.

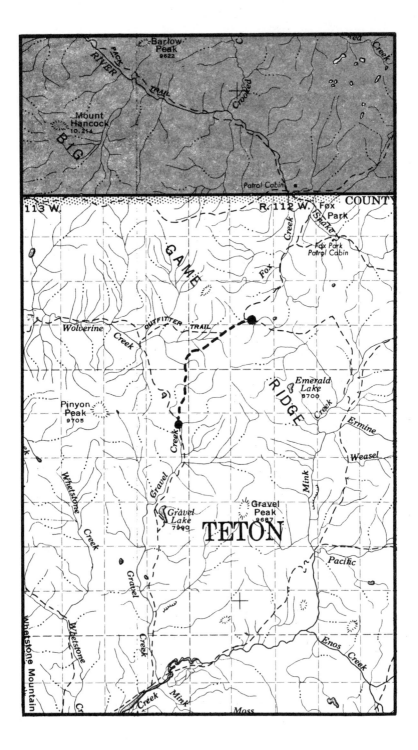

At the junction which ends the Gravel Creek Trail, you stand in a pretty meadow, decorated with small groves of trees and a pond. Rugged Pinyon Peak thrusts up to the West. This steep mountain is composed of conglomerate. Erosion from its slopes has contributed most of the rock in Gravel Creek. The gentler rise to the north is the start of Big Game Ridge. The Big Game Ridge Cutoff Trail climbs over the low southern end of Big Game Ridge to join with the Snake River and the Mink Creek Cutoff trail after three miles.

The trail climbs out of the meadow passing across mostly open slopes. Here is a fine view down Gravel Creek and a photographer's must of ragged Pinyon Peak. After an ascent of perhaps 400 feet, you reach a flat through which a small stream flows. Next, is a climb of 200 feet while heading around to the backside of the ridge. Here the trail levels out in the deep woods of a northwest-facing slope. Soon you hike out of the forest and shortly make the climb to a gentle and pretty pass. At the pass a sign points to a faint trail to the left that cuts over to Wolverine Creek. This is an outfitter's trail. It is hard to follow and not described in this book.

You begin to descend the other side of the pass and in about ¼ mile you come to another sign at a trail junction. The more used of the two trails (the one to your left) is the Snake River Trail. It leads to Fox Park and then winds far northwestward into Yellowstone Park following the infant Snake River all the way to the southern entrance of that national park. The right fork is the Mink Creek Cut-off Trail, a little used path that takes you into the Mink Creek Burn country.

6b WOLVERINE CREEK

Length: 4½ miles.
Effort: 5 miles to Trail 3c; 5½ miles from
Trail 3c to Trail 6.
Trail condition: Fair to poor.
River crossings: Four, July 1.
Trail use: Very light.
Topographic Quadrangle: Mt. Hancock.

This is a pretty trail into remote, little-known country. It goes about 4½ miles down the creek where it joins with little used Trail 3c. Maps show the trail going all the way to the end of Wolverine Creek in

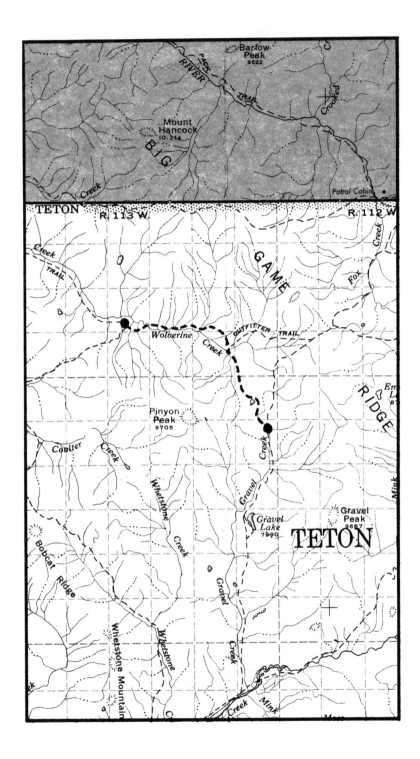

Yellowstone Park. This part of the trail should be considered dead for trail hiking purposes, although a cross country hike would not be really difficult.

Begin at the end of the Gravel Creek Trail (Trail 6). Walk through the lovely meadow, crossing a small headwater tributary of Wolverine Creek. In ¼ mile you cross another small creek. If you follow this creek just a little way upstream you reach a scenic little lake surrounded by forest and meadowland.

Now you descend 400 feet and cross Wolverine Creek. All fords of Wolverine Creek and its tributaries are easy by the time of the year people can get this deep into the Teton Wilderness (July 15–20).

Wolverine Creek immediately tumbles into a canyon. To avoid it, the trail climbs 200 feet through forest, descends to cross a tributary creek, and then it passes a pond heading through forest for a mile to a big meadow through which Wolverine Creek meanders lazily amid piles of river gravel.

At the edge of the meadow, you ford Wolverine Creek. On the other side the trail is poor, having been nearly flooded out by the beaver. Cross the meadow and then skirt through timber and cross over a small creek. Leave the timber and cross another tiny creek. Very soon past this point you pick up the Rodent-Wolverine Trail (Number 3c) that leads from here up the forested ridge to your left.

7 MINK CREEK

Length: 17 miles.
Effort: 20 miles from Pacific Creek to
*   Bridger Lake via Phelps Pass; 19½*
*   miles the opposite direction.*
Trail condition: Mostly good to fair, one
*   short poor section.*
River crossings: Numerous, August 1 for
*   the Yellowstone River.*
Trail use: Very light until late July, medium
*   thereafter.*
Topographic Quadrangles: Mt. Hancock,
*   Two Ocean Pass.*

This lengthy trail takes you from Pacific Creek to famous Bridger Lake and the Yellowstone Meadows (or vice-versa) by way of Mink

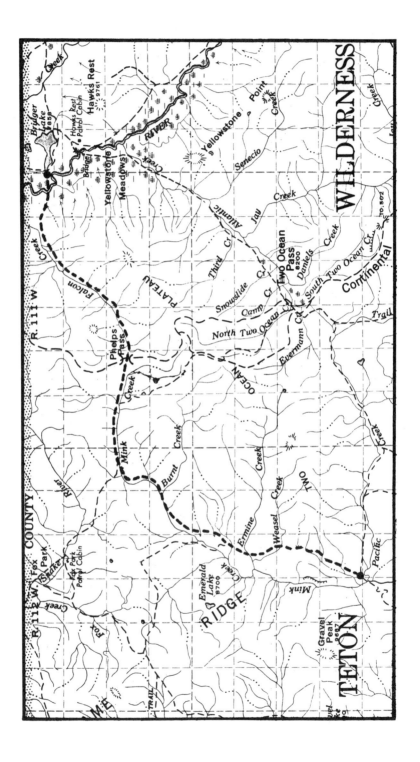

Creek and Falcon Creek. It is a pretty trip, but it isn't as favored by folks as the route over Two Ocean Pass due to its greater distance and the difficult ford of the Yellowstone River at the bottom of Falcon Creek. The trail also provides an alternate access route to Fox Park over Trail Number 7a.

Use of the Mink Creek Trail is very low until about the end of July. Once the Yellowstone River is fordable, use picks up considerably. You can get into Mink Creek as early as July 1, however, if you come in on the Enos Lake Trail (Trail 9).

Most of lower Mink Creek was the site of a large fire in the 1930s. The Mink Creek Burn actually started in Gravel Creek. It spread to Mink Creek and went through 13,000 acres of thick timber. It is adjoined on the north by the 4000 acre Fox Park Burn, which burned in 1940. Today lodgepole pine is reclaiming most of these burns. Some of the new trees now stand over thirty feet high, but the snags, blackened stumps, and numerous open patches give mute testimony to this large fire. I guess that the Mink Creek country is probably more interesting to travel through than it was before the fire. The landscape is rather subdued, but views are not blocked by trees. I don't know if wildlife is more abundant, but I've seen more game here than in most parts of the Wilderness. Deer, elk, and moose are very frequently visible.

The trail up Mink Creek begins about half way up the climb out of Pacific Creek, just after the difficult Mink Creek ford. For those coming down Pacific Creek, a spur leaves Trail 4 about a mile above (east) of the Mink Creek crossing. This trail is unsigned, but it is obvious. It leaves, heading to the northwest, just as you emerge from the trees into a large meadow. This trail joins the other at a signed junction about one-half mile up Mink Creek.

At first, the Mink Creek Trail leads through flat meadow country. It then climbs steeply 200 feet to a plateau and you enter the Burn. Here a dense forest of lodgepole is rapidly reclaiming the land. Mink Creek itself is over ¾ of a mile to the west where it plunges through an impassable gorge.

The trail crosses tributary Weasel Creek, which you can usually hop over on rocks. Then it drops 200 feet to Ermine Creek, which is larger, but no problem. You are now north of the start of the Mink Creek gorge, and you can follow Ermine Creek down to Mink Creek (a quarter mile) if you wish. Mink Creek looks as if it should be excellent fishing, but I've never even got a bite or seen a fish. Mink Creek is lined with willows here, and there are lots of moose.

The nearly level trail heads north from Ermine Creek crossing. Soon you cross a nice, but often damp, meadow. Jump a small unnamed stream and just to the other side a definite trail leaves to your left. As of July 1977, there was no sign, but I believe that the Forest

Service erected one late in 1977. At any rate, the trail to the left is the Mink Creek Cut-off Trail (Number 7b).

Beyond the trail junction you pass through mostly open landscape, not yet reclaimed by trees despite the years since the burn. Some times of the year the flowers along here are very beautiful. As you continue northward, the walls of a canyon rise up in front of you. Here, approximately where Burnt Creek runs in, the trail passes through some very mushy areas. The trail's condition is quite poor, but you will not get lost because, for the first time, the trail follows Mink Creek closely. Just keep following the stream until the trail leads you into the canyon ahead. Notice that the walls of the canyon are volcanic. You are now out of the sedimentary Pinyon Peak Highlands and in the Absaroka Mountains.

The canyon is short in length. Soon you are in the upper part of Mink Creek, characterized by a gentle grade and low-growing willows along the creek. Just on the other side of a ford of Mink Creek (not much water but slippery rocks), a sign marks the beginning of Trail 7a. This leads through the Fox Park Burn and along the headwaters of the Snake River to Fox Park. You have to watch for this junction because the trail continues up the right (south side) of Mink Creek as well. The Trail 7a junction is just a little way above the end of the Mink Creek Burn.

From here the trail continues up a gentle, open stream valley. In a mile you meet the Two Ocean Plateau Trail where two brooks blend their waters to form Mink Creek. All the willows and meadows here make it look like bear country—and it is. From here it is just a short way to Phelps Pass.

Phelps Pass (8750 feet) is a broad gentle summit with the Two Ocean Plateau rising on both sides. Although it isn't nearly as level as Two Ocean Pass, four linear miles to the south, these two passes have a similar origin. Thousands of years ago the Yellowstone Valley to the east was filled with glaciers to the depth of several thousand feet. The depth of the ice rose from the top of the valley northward to the site of Yellowstone Lake. Since the normal northward drainage was blocked during this frigid time, melt waters rose until they flowed over the Two Ocean Plateau and to the west. Two Ocean Pass, Phelps Pass, and the head of Lynx Creek (to the north in Yellowstone) were low spots through which the icy torrent poured. For a time this region drained into the ancestral Snake River. As the glaciers melted, their level dropping, first Lynx Creek, then Phelps Pass, and finally, Two Ocean Pass, were abandoned. In each case the passes were left much deeper than before the ice age.

Phelps Pass marks the Continental Divide. Just down the other side you step across a tiny stream—the start of Falcon Creek.

The grade downhill increases as you follow Falcon Creek through forest with some open spots. The trail emerges into a long riparian

Mink Creek near the confluence of Burnt Creek.

meadow and soon the grade becomes less. Falcon Creek meanders through the middle. After a mile the trail returns to forest. One more mile and the grade becomes quite steep as you leave the creek's side and cut directly down through forest to Yellowstone Meadows. The massive Trident stands to the northeast across this broad valley. Hawks Rest Mountain is the singular peak to the southeast.

Dead ahead is the Yellowstone River, a tough crossing any time of the year. Usually you can make it after the first week in August. If

The Mink Creek Burn 45 years later.

not, you can find a place upstream or downstream where the stream is wider. Once across, it is only a third of a mile to famous Bridger Lake. If you are on horseback, you should know that no grazing is allowed within a half mile of Bridger Lake. It's just too popular.

There are almost unlimited campsites throughout Yellowstone Meadows. You don't have to camp with the crowds at the lake. Fishing is just as fabulous in the Yellowstone River as it is at the lake.

At the lake, a trail leaves to the north. This trail is ¾ of a mile to Yellowstone Park. You need a fishing permit to fish there and a back-country permit to camp. These are available at the Park Service's Thorofare Ranger Station, two miles northeast from Bridger Lake, across Thorofare Creek (another fun ford), at the base of the Trident.

Moose are extremely abundant through the upper valley of the Yellowstone River. Early in the Summer there are lots of bears. They come to feed on the spawning cutthroat trout.

7a NORTH MINK CREEK CUT-OFF

Length: 3½ miles.
Effort: 4 miles from Mink Creek to Fox Park Patrol Cabin; 4½ miles from the patrol cabin to Mink Creek.
Trail condition: Fair.
River crossings: Two, July 1.
Trail use: Very low.

This is the best way to get to Fox Park from Mink Creek, although Trail 7b will also do the trick.

The trail begins at a sign just beyond a ford of Mink Creek. You climb out of the canyon of Mink Creek while passing in and out of the Fox Park Burn (from the year 1940), and you finally pass over a low place on the Two Ocean Plateau. The climb is about 300 feet. From the plateau, you can see a meadow below as you gaze through the burnt snags and vigorous new forest. When you drop down to the meadow, there is a creek meandering through it, hidden in a maze of willows. The creek, just a little too large to jump, is the "mighty" Snake River only four miles from its source. You can bushwhack your way to the Snake's origin high on a grassy slope of the Two Ocean Plateau on the Wilderness/Yellowstone Park boundary.

The baby Snake River rushes through Fox Park and turns northward into Yellowstone, picking up water rapidly. Next, it turns south and flows out of Yellowstone and soon into Jackson Lake, the first of many reservoirs. In theory, the Snake eventually weds its waters with those of the Columbia River. In fact the Snake dries up almost every Summer below Milner Dam in southern Idaho—its waters spent on irrigation. Idaho developers like to call the Snake "a working river." People like these give unemployment a good name.

After you cross the Snake, pass through the woods a short distance. Then recross the Snake. Stomp through more willows and shortly you arrive at the Fox Park Patrol Cabin. This is a big cabin, but it's usually not occupied. A cold spring emerges behind the cabin.

Adjacent is Fox Park, the meeting place of many trails and many creeks. Wildlife is abundant, but striking scenery is lacking. Fox Park is a large oval-shaped meadow with beautiful flowers in mid-Summer, but it is surrounded by featureless forested hills.

I usually have an excellent sense of direction in the wilderness, but Fox Park is a place I had to consult my compass to get my directions straight.

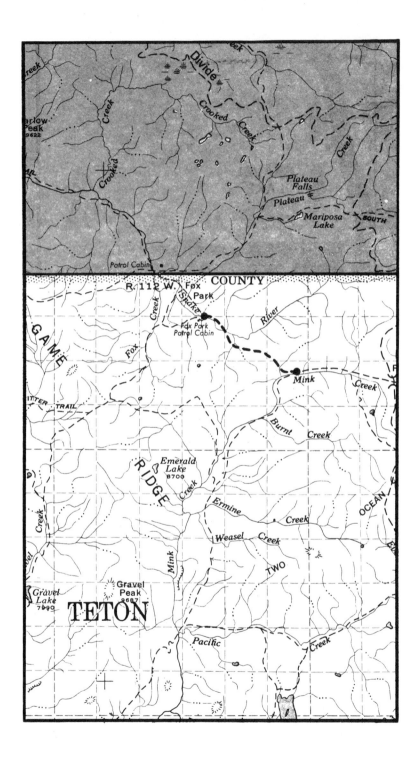

Camping is good at Fox Park, and just west of Fox Park there are a series of unnamed meadows waiting for you to explore. The hill that rises to the west of Fox Park is actually Big Game Ridge. It doesn't look like much, but it is over 10,000 feet high and involves a lengthy hike to the top.

7b MINK CREEK CUT-OFF

Length: 5 miles.
Effort: 7 miles from Mink Creek to the Big
*   Game Ridge Cut-off Trail; 5 ½ miles the*
*   opposite direction.*
Trail condition: Fair to poor.
River crossings: One, July 15.
Trail use: Very low.
Topographic Quadrangle: Mt. Hancock.

This is a seldom-used path leading up out of Mink Creek and into the headwaters of Fox Creek where it ends at the junction of the Big Game Ridge Cut-off and the Snake River Trail.

On the Mink Creek Trail (Number 7) just after you have crossed Ermine Creek, you will find a low hill to your left and the more substantial (yet gentle) rise of the Two Ocean Plateau to your right. You soon come to a nice, flat meadow and cross a lazily-flowing creek. Just on the other side of the creek an obvious trail leaves to your left (west) at a sign. If you climb a tiny hill and go past an outfitter's camp, you have gone too far. Turn back.

The Mink Creek Cut-off descends to Mink Creek and crosses it in a narrow stream valley filled with willows. Look for moose. You should be able to make the ford after about July 15.

The trail climbs 600 feet up an open hillside (that way since the Mink Creek Burn). At the top, you head into forest and then you come to the edge of a nice, wet meadow. Here is a trail junction and a sign. The trail to the right leads to Fox Park. The Mink Creek Cut-off continues to the left and climbs another 40 feet to the top of a forested plateau and then it falls 200 feet steeply to a pass at the head of Fox Creek and an unnamed tributary of Mink Creek. To your right (the north), infant Fox Creek twists through a lovely mile-long meadow. From here you climb 400 feet through the woods part way up Big Game Ridge to the signed junction of Trails 7c and 6a.

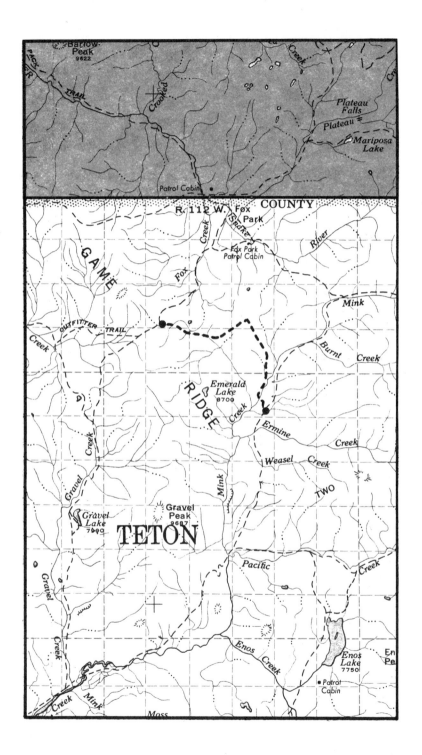

Fox Park.

The Fox Park Burn as seen from the North Mink Creek Cut-off trail.

Beginnings of the mighty Snake River.

7c SNAKE RIVER

Length: 4 miles plus 18 more north in
    Yellowstone Park.
Effort: 5½ miles from Yellowstone south to
    the Big Game Ridge trail.
Trail condition: Fair.
River crossings: Two, July 10.
Trail use: Low.
Topographic Quadrangle: Mt. Hancock.

One might say, this trail and the Big Game Ridge Cutoff Trail are continuations of the Gravel Creek Trail. Most folks heading to Fox

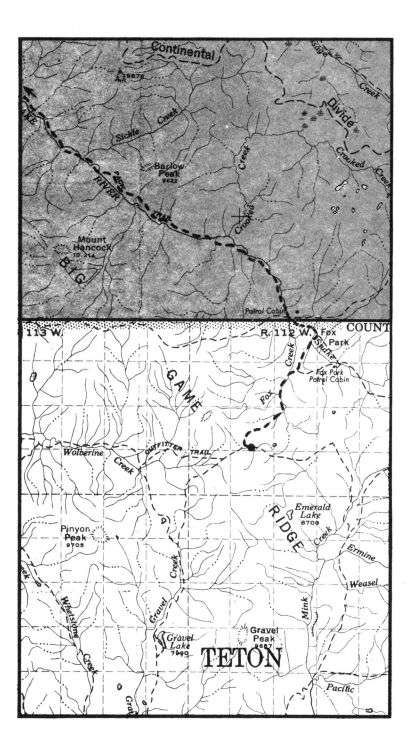

Remote Fox Creek.

Park come this way. There are many miles of this trail continuing northward into Yellowstone Park. In the Park, the trail follows the growing Snake River closely, winding through canyons and past hot springs. There it crosses the Snake River many times.

The Big Game Ridge Cutoff Trail ends on the east side of Big Game Ridge. The Snake River Trail is the one to the west at the trail junction. It descends all the way down Big Game Ridge to Fox Creek through forest. It follows Fox Creek for a mile, crossing several of its tributaries, then it crosses Fox Creek (no problem). A climb of about 80 feet brings you to the spacious meadow called Fox Park. The trail keeps to the extreme west side of this meadow and crosses the Snake River at the meadow's northern terminus. From here it is a hop and a skip through the trees to Yellowstone Park. The so-called South Boundary Trail, which you meet, offers a pretty route to Yellowstone Meadows by going over the Two Ocean Plateau and past meadowy and good fishing Mariposa Lake, then down Lynx Creek. The Snake River Trail itself takes a jog to the west and then plunges north, deep into the Park.

7d SOUTH BOUNDARY

Length: 16 miles.
Effort: 22 miles from Wolverine Creek to
  Fox Park; 19½ miles the opposite
  direction.
Trail condition: Good.
River crossings: Two, August 1 for
  Wolverine Creek.
Trail use: Low.
Topographic Quadrangles: Huckleberry
  Mountain, Mt Hancock.

This trail is a really long climb, but it goes through outstanding big game country (especially elk range), and the top of Big Game Ridge gives the best panoramic view from a trail in the entire Teton Wilderness. There are a few places to camp about halfway down this trail's east side, but otherwise you pretty much have to do it all in one day. The climb out of Wolverine Creek is longer than the one from Fox Park. In fact, it's a real bitch. We did the whole thing from Wolverine Creek to Fox Park in one day. I've never been more tired.

Most of the South Boundary Trail is in Yellowstone National Park, and I haven't described it due to its lack of relation to the Teton Wilderness, but the portion over Big Game Ridge wanders in and out of the Teton Wilderness. Nevertheless, the Park Service considers it their trail and their rules apply. A Park Ranger caught us on the trail with a dog. For a minute I thought he was going to call in the helicopters from Old Faithful, but we convinced him we were just stragglers from the Wilderness Area who would depart with haste once we were on the other side of the ridge. I don't know why management of this common border isn't better coordinated between the Park Service and the Forest Service, but any reading of the history of the public lands indicates that the Forest Service and the Park Service don't waste any love on each other.

Let's describe the trail from Wolverine Creek. Camp either downstream or upstream (depending on where you came from and whether you have a Park Service backcountry permit). There are lots of places to camp along Wolverine Creek or nearby Snake River. In either case you must ford Wolverine Creek to reach the trail. This isn't easy until at least mid-Summer. The trail is unsigned, but its beginning is distinct. It begins just after the ford of Wolverine Creek inside the Park, or, alternatively (if you are coming upstream), just after the

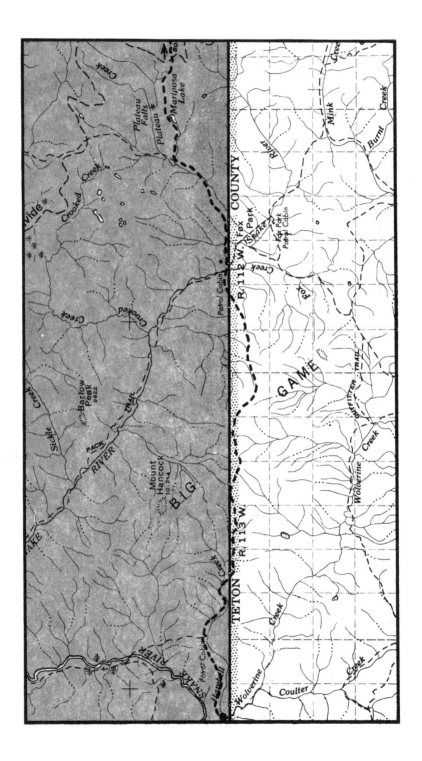

first ford of Wolverine Creek and before the second. Wolverine Creek is the large stream that runs into the Snake River. You will know for sure when you are on the South Boundary Trail because the Park identifies all of their trails with orange metal tags attached to trees.

The trail climbs gently through meadows and forest, then passes through dry lodgepole woods. In several miles you arrive at the Park Service's Harebell Patrol Cabin. Don't take the trail to the north. This heads to the Snake River. The trail to the right is the correct one. The trail follows Harebell Creek closely after you pass the Park Service Cabin. In addition, once you are past the cabin, the trail climbs continuously. Harebell Creek is crossed several times, with no difficulty.

Hike through dense spruce and fir forest along the creek. We found the mosquitos intense and saw many signs of bear. The trail seems to get even steeper and the forest thicker until it finally levels out just before the upper crossing of Harebell Creek. There are some marginal campsites here. The trail leads you around a pond in a forest primeval setting. Now it is time to prepare for the final pitch—a steep, continuous 1400 foot climb through the woods. There isn't a good view until you break into the open and the trail flattens out at an elevation of about 9900 feet. When the view comes you can't help but be impressed.

The trail rambles at timberline for about 3 miles over the top of the ridge. Because you cross at a high point on the ridge there is a nearly 360 degree view. As you cross the ridge, look northward into Yellowstone across a deep, unnamed canyon through which the Snake River flows. Beyond that you see Heart Lake and Yellowstone Lake. Still further lies the forested Mirror Plateau, the northern boundary of Yellowstone, and the Absaroka and Gallatin Ranges in Montana. To the east (from left to right), stretches the craggy outline of the Absaroka Mountains, over a hundred miles in length.

Southward your view soars over the Pinyon Peak Highlands. It flies further to the Mt. Leidy Highlands, finally resting on the wild peaks of the Gros Ventres. Far to the south you can see the Snake River Range; and, to the distant southeast, a bit of the mighty Wind Rivers. To the West, the Tetons rake the sky. Just north of them you can make out the Henry's Lake Mountains on the Idaho-Montana border, while in the foreground is the forested Pitchstone Plateau of Yellowstone.

Few places in the West command such a view. Big Game Ridge itself seems to be adequately protected, but how long the view will last, given the intent of the giant utilities to fill the West with huge, smoke-belching powerplants, is anyone's guess. As you enjoy the view, ask yourself what you've personally done to earn such a sight. Have you expressed your views to politicians, joined any conservation organizations, or given time or money in the battle against those who degrade our wilderness areas?

The ridgetop is covered with sparse grass and forbs between the patches of whitebark pine. As you cross the ridge, you are likely to see elk. Possibly you'll spot other wilderness species such as bear as well. A wolverine was recently spotted on Big Game Ridge. The ridge's name is not misleading. There are some flat places to camp on top, but they are not recommended since there is usually no water and the ridge is susceptible to violent storms.

The descent down the east side of Big Game Ridge is not as long as the ascent of the ridge's west side, although it is a substantial hike. The eastern side's scenery is more varied with quite a few open spots and small, often wet, meadows. From July until mid-August, the open places are often tinged purple from the many lupines that bloom. There are places to camp on the east side, but few of them are of high quality.

The trail drops the last 200 feet steeply, entering Yellowstone in a meadow that adjoins the small Snake River just northwest of Fox Park. Our description of this trail ends where it meets the Snake River Trail, just past the ford of the Snake (July 15). The South Boundary Trail continues eastward, however, a few miles inside Yellowstone Park, going past pretty Mariposa Lake, down Lynx Creek, and ending at Yellowstone Meadows.

Note: the meadows in and around Fox Park are perhaps the prime grizzly concentration area in the Teton Wilderness.

8 LAVA CREEK

Length: 9½ miles.
Effort: 13 miles.
Trail condition: Poor.
River crossings: One, July 1.
Trail use: Very low.
Topographic Quadrangles: Davis Hill,
   Whetstone Mountain, Gravel Mountain.

This is the least-used of the entrances to the Teton Wilderness, and while Lava Creek doesn't lie deep inside the Teton Wilderness, it could be a hundred miles from the road for all the use it gets. It's not that Lava Creek is unattractive. It is very interesting with curious Gravel Mountain rising above the beautiful Lava Creek Meadows. The

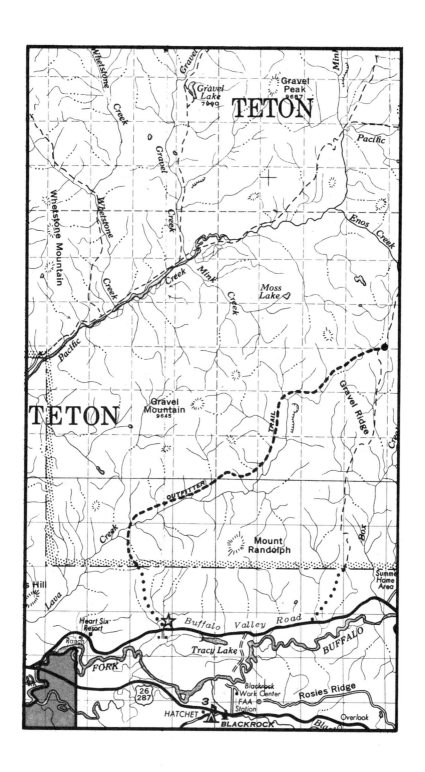

problem, I think (if you consider lack of use a problem), is that the hiker is greeted by a drab-looking trailhead and an uneventful 1500 foot climb and a long descent before reaching Lava Creek.

To get to the trailhead, turn right at Moran Junction and head east toward Dubois on U.S. 26/287. In about 4 miles, a green sign announces the Buffalo Valley Road to the left. The Lava Creek trailhead is four-and-one-half miles down this narrow, paved road. A small sign identifies the spot. There is room to park one car in the open right next to the paved road.

The trail climbs steadily through sagebrush for about 300 feet and ¼ mile until you enter first aspen and then conifer forest. There are some nice views of the Tetons and the Buffalo River Valley from the first part of this trail (the aspen in the fall make an excellent frame for a photograph).

You continue to climb almost continuously for two more miles through forest until the top is reached at 8500 feet elevation (the trailhead is 6871 feet). From the top, the trail drops 1000 continuous feet through a solid forest canopy to Lava Creek. Here you enter the pretty and spacious Lava Creek Meadows with a ford of Lava Creek. The ford is deep but slow; you can ford the creek after about the first of July. Ragged, strange-looking Gravel Mountain (elevation 9636 feet) rises to the north of the meadows. This mountain is a pile of conglomerate. All the streams that drain Gravel Mountain are wide swaths of gravel—a contrast to the gently-flowing, and bank-full, Lava Creek as it meanders through the 4-mile long meadow.

The trail crosses a major tributary of Lava Creek just after the Lava Creek ford. This creek drains the "ravelled" slopes of Gravel Mountain. It's full of rocks.

For the next four miles the trail follows the north side of the meadows, crossing an occasional small tributary stream. There are many places to camp. Lava Creek is good fishing for small trout, and the numerous ponds in the meadow create excellent waterfowl and moose habitat.

At meadow's end the trail climbs 200 feet through forest and open slopes to an upper meadow of Lava Creek. This flower-strewn meadow is smaller than the lower. It's narrower and about 1½ miles long. There is good camping here as well. The steep hill to the south is Gravel Ridge (not to be confused with Gravel Mountain or Gravel Peak in the Mink Creek country). The trail is faint through the upper meadow. If you lose it, keep walking to the upper end of the meadow. Keep near to the lowest part. You should find the trail as it enters the forest at the end of the meadow. If not, walk eastward cross country through the forest. In an eighth of a mile you will come to the easily-identified Enos Lake Trail (Number 9). If you are on Trail 9 and looking for the Lava Creek Trail, here's how to find it. Coming from Enos Lake (i.e., Southward on the Enos Lake Trail), you pass a small log-filled pond (it goes dry in late Summer). Just the other side a faint trail leaves to the right (west). This is it. Just a little way further you get a second chance in case you missed the first. This time the trail has a sign, but only for those coming northward up the trail.

Mt. Leidy and the Buffalo Valley from the start of the Lava Creek trail.

9   ENOS LAKE

Length: 10 miles.
Effort: 12½ miles from the Box Creek
     trailhead to Enos Creek; 11 miles the
     opposite direction.
Trail condition: Good to fair.
River crossings: None.
Trail use: Medium.
Topographic Quadrangles: Rosies Ridge,
     Gravel Mountain.

This is a major route to popular Enos Lake, the largest lake in the Teton Wilderness. The Enos Lake Trail does not offer any bold

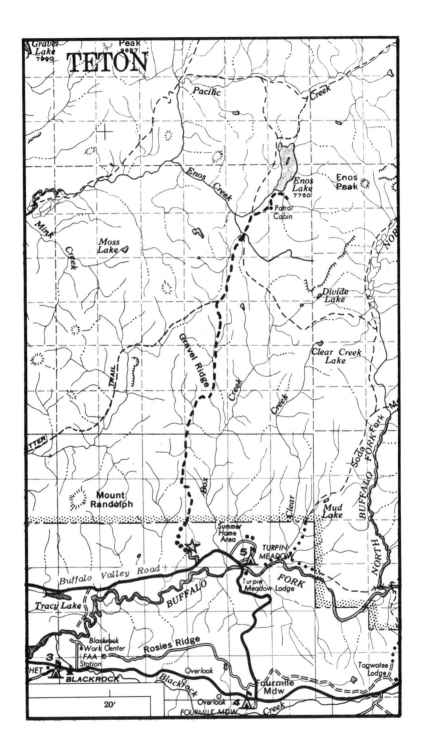

scenery, but it is open relatively early in the season, providing access to Enos Lake and the land northward.

The Box Creek trailhead is the start of the Enos Lake Trail. You drive about 9 miles down the Buffalo Valley Road to an obvious sign identifying the trailhead. This is just before the road crossing of Box Creek. It is important to note that this trailhead was recently re-located. It used to be about a mile further back on the road (west). The most recent USGS topographic quadrangle, Rosies Ridge (1965) shows the trailhead in the old place. You can still use the old trailhead, but parking is better at the new one.

At the road sign identifying the new trailhead, a dirt road leads 0.7 miles to the actual trailhead. Here there is ample parking and a trail register.

View up the South Fork of the Buffalo Canyon from the Enos Lake trail.

Down Box Creek from Gravel Ridge.

The first part of this trail is similar to the Lava Creek Trail (Number 8). You climb continuously, at first through a sagebrush and grass-covered hillside with patches of aspen, and, increasingly, fir and pine. Eventually you enter deep forest, still climbing, with few views and no water. In June the beginning of the trip is actually quite pleasant with many flowers blooming in the sagebrush and grass. The aspen is very green with new leaves, and you can spot many deer, especially at the transition between the sagebrush and the forest. In late Summer, I find this trip rather monotonous. There are some nice views of the Buffalo River Valley at the start of the trail. The forested mountains to the south are the Mt. Leidy Highlands, and until a few years ago, this was a large expanse of **de facto** wilderness. Now the Forest Service is busy dissecting the area with timber roads. The

86

forest the trail winds through will never be logged, however. It is protected by an Act of Congress, even though many of the large trees are what the timber industry likes to term as "over-mature," "decadent," and grow in patches that are not "thrifty."

These old trees creak and groan in the wind, and walking through this dense forest can at times give you the willys when you are alone.

The trail stops climbing after 2½ miles. For the next mile you walk horizontally along a densely-forested bench located on the side of a ridge. Finally you break out into a large meadow through which runs a small stream. Some people mistakenly think the stream is Box Creek, but instead it is one of its tributaries (the trail never crosses Box Creek). The low ridge you see ahead is Gravel Ridge.

About ¼ mile further on in a patch of woods on the meadow's edge, a trail leaves to the left. There is no sign. Be sure to stay to the right since the left fork is an unmaintained path that goes on the "wrong" (west) side of Gravel Ridge and then leads into Lava Creek. Once we met a large party at Enos Lake that had taken this fork of the trail by mistake, spending a day wandering in confusion as a result.

The Enos Lake Trail turns at a right angle just past the above-mentioned fork and follows the base of Gravel Ridge for ¼ mile. It then turns northward and abruptly climbs the 300 feet to the open ridgetop. Here are the best views on the Enos Lake Trail. This means a fair view of oddly-formed Gravel Mountain two miles to your west and a good view down into trailless Box Creek. Eastward a few peaks of the Absarokas jut above the smooth ridgeline seen on the other side of Box Creek.

The trail gradually descends the other side of Gravel Ridge, passing through the pleasant meadows that line a headwater of Box Creek. There are some campsites here and a few trout in the stream. At times this meadow provides a fine flower show.

After about two more miles you pass over a gentle divide located in the woods. Just on the other side, and just past a small log-filled pond, the Lava Creek Trail (Number 8) leaves to the left (i.e., the west). There is a small sign on the base of a large tree that identifies this faint path.

The Enos Lake Trail next descends steeply, losing about 120 feet elevation while it drops through a thick, damp forest on a northward-facing slope. The trail continues its descent, but less abruptly. Soon it crosses several small linear meadows. The trail drops into a small canyon and crosses two creeks. At the first creek, the Divide Trail (Number 10a) joins the Enos Lake Trail. Note that the USGS Gravel Mountain quadrangle incorrectly shows the Divide Trail as joining at the second creek. Fortunately, this potentially confusing junction sported a good trail sign when last observed.

When you climb out of this small canyon, you find yourself in the broad meadows just south of Enos Lake. Soon the trail forks. If your aim is the south shore of the lake, take the trail to the right. The sign for this route reads "Enos Lake Patrol Cabin, ½ mile."

The broader left fork quickly crosses a stream (Enos Creek), and here a second junction occurs. The right fork bears the inscription, "Pacific Creek 3, Two Ocean Pass 8, Yellowstone River 15." The sign for the left fork reads, "Enos Creek Outfitter Trail" and "Pacific Creek." Thus, both trails will take you to Pacific Creek, but the left fork reaches Pacific Creek much further downstream. The Enos Creek Outfitter Trail is Number 9a. The right fork is 9b.

The remainder of the trip to Enos Lake (via the right-hand trail at the first fork encountered) is a gentle hike through a meadow, past the patrol cabin and then through forest to the lakeshore. The patrol cabin isn't usually occupied. There is a nice cold spring in the trees just behind the cabin.

Enos Lake is a good place to fish and to see moose. On my last trip there I saw 14 moose in two days. The trout are mostly medium-sized and abundant. My first view of Enos Lake filled me with great expectations of fishing. The waters were literally filled with fish, kind of orange-colored, but very numerous. Closer inspection sadly revealed, however, that these orange fish were big, fat and ugly Utah Chubs. They infest the smallow waters that ring the lake in large numbers. Unless you wade through these squeeshy margins of the lake, you are much more likely to catch these critters than trout. If you do hook one, for heaven's sakes, don't throw it back. Kill it, and then there will be one less, at least temporarily.

The bad things about Enos Lake are the Chubs, the soft mud all the way around the lake, and the fact that sometimes it's kind of crowded (both people and mosquitos). But the lake also has an exquisite beauty, set between two ridges that are covered with spruce and flowered meadows. The graceful lines of two trumpeter swans usually help decorate the fertile waters of the lake. If you can find a campsite near the lake, and there aren't many, you may have the treat of seeing moose swim past your tent.

Although there are only a few good camping spots next to the lake, there are plenty nearby. If you follow the south shore trail to its end, you will find a really nice spot near a cold stream with a view out over the willows to the lake. Nearby another small stream tumbles over a cliff. I once spent a pleasant evening here entertaining a preacher and his companions with tales of the hungry grizzly bears nearby. Interestingly, I've met quite a few men of the cloth in these woods. For all their talk about heaven, they're just as worried about being eaten as anyone else. Actually there is little to worry about. Clean your camp, hang your food, pour a shot of whiskey, and forget about the bears.

9a ENOS CREEK OUTFITTER

Length: 3½ miles.
Effort: 4 miles from either direction.
Trail condition: Poor.
River crossings: Two, August 1 for Pacific
*   Creek.*
Trail use: Very light.
Topographic Quadrangle: Gravel Mountain.

Also known as the Enos Creek Cut-off Trail, this path leads you through gentle, open, and willowy meadows along Enos Creek and also across a scenic, but seldom-visited canyon of Pacific Creek. The trail provides a short cut from the Pacific Creek Trail (Number 4) to Enos Lake or vice-versa.

Here's the description beginning on Trail 4. The trail begins at a signed junction in a tiny meadow lying about a mile east of the head of the big Pacific Creek Meadows. Pacific Creek, its streamside scenery ever-changing, emerges from an untrailed canyon a short distance south of this small meadow. By the way, the top end of this canyon is near the confluence of Pacific and Mink Creek.

Trail Number 9a crosses a tiny tributary creek, then climbs steeply 200 feet through the forest to a plateau. Next it slowly descends into the aforementioned gorge of Pacific Creek. Occasionally open side slopes provide good views of this steep (but not really deep) canyon. The crossing of Pacific Creek in the bottom of the canyon is a matter of some excitement. As of August 1, the river is 2½ or 3 feet deep, moderately swift, and full of oddly-shaped and slippery rocks near mid-stream. You absolutely must wear tennis shoes to cross safely. Take your time, measure each step, and you'll make it.

Just past this ford you cross the mouth of Enos Creek, an easy crossing. From here you start up a canyon cut by Enos Creek, but the canyon soon opens up into a broad stream valley covered by willows. Enos Creek winds gracefully through this valley. Look for moose. A creek flows into Enos Creek from the southern end of the stream valley. You may think this is the direction the trail will take, but suddenly Enos Creek, and the trail, makes a sharp left turn toward the east. Watch carefully so that you don't miss this bend in the trail.

From the bend, the trail climbs gently for a mile or so, following Enos Creek through patches of forest, but mostly through meadows filled with flowers and willows. The topography is gentle. There are quite a few springs running across the trail until late in the Summer.

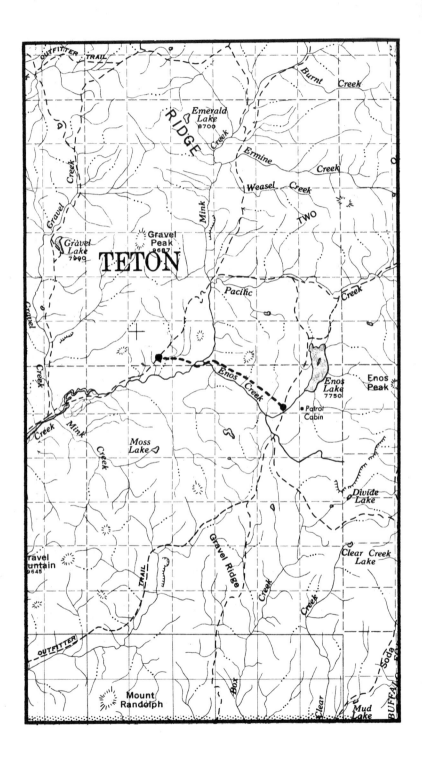

The stream valley gradually becomes broader and increasingly covered with low-growing willows (kept that way by moose). You may lose the trail. If so, climb the north side of the stream valley (about 200 feet), and you'll find the trail wending its way over a gently-rolling bench. Often the bench is covered with a riot of flowers. Soon you reach the junction of Trails 9 and 9a at the crossing of Enos Creek about a mile below the south end of Enos Lake.

9b CONTINUATION OF ENOS LAKE

Length: 2½ miles.
Effort: 3 miles from either end.
Trail condition: Fair.
River crossings: None.
Trail use: Medium.
Topographic Quadrangles: Two Ocean
    Pass, Gravel Mountain.

Beginning at the junction of the Enos Creek Outfitter Trail at Enos Creek (about a half mile south of Enos Lake), is what I consider to be a separate trail from Trail Number 9 described earlier. The Gravel Mtn. Quadrangle does label it the Enos Lake Trail, however. I guess it really doesn't matter.

The trail slowly angles away from Enos Creek and its willowy path meanders and climbs the ridge to the west of Enos Lake. It climbs about 200 feet, which is half-way to the ridgetop, and provides fine views of tranquil Enos Lake as you pass through openings in the forest.

The trail slowly descends to near the lakeshore. Here numerous hummocks begin to appear near the north end of the lake. The northern end of the lake has an irregular outline and is more scenic than the southern end, I think. There are also more places to camp. The volcanic Two Ocean Plateau looms closer and closer as you tramp northward past the end of the lake. This contrasts with the white, obviously sedimentary rock that constitutes the many hillocks.

Trail 9c leaves to the right at the top of the lake. This trail is but a ½ mile walk through forest and meadows to Pacific Creek.

Trail 9b climbs "over hill and dale" past a number of ponds set among these curious swales. Flowers and small groves of spruce and

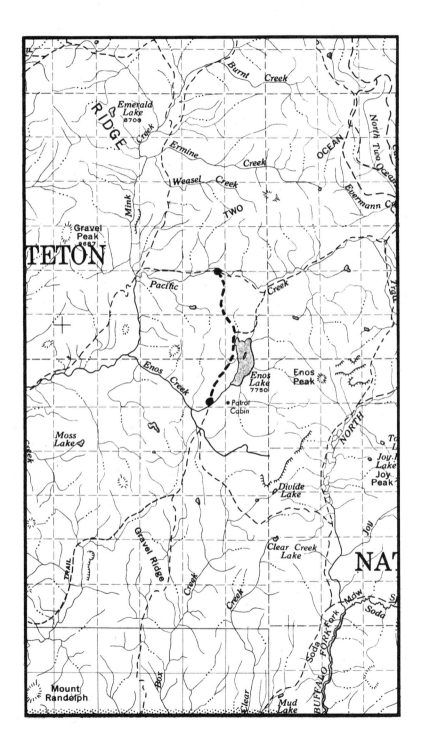

fir bedeck the landscape. You may surprise game here because the horizon is limited by the many hummocks. After about a third of a mile, you begin to descend in to Pacific Creek. You walk around a northward-facing slope (kind of damp), and follow a trickle of water down to the Pacific Creek Trail (Number 4).

10   CLEAR CREEK
(also known as the Turner Cut-off)

Length: 7 miles.
Effort: 10 miles.
Trail condition: Fair to poor, finally fading
out.
River crossings: Several, minor.
Trail use: Light.
Topographic Quadrangles: Rosies Ridge,
Gravel Mountain, Joy Peak

This trail, in combination with the Divide Creek Trail (Number 10b), provides a more scenic route to Enos Lake than does the Enos Lake Trail (Number 9). Happily the route is not longer, yet it does get less use because it lacks a developed trailhead. In addition, it is described poorly on the maps. I much prefer this trail to Trail 9.

To get to the trailhead, take the Buffalo Valley Road and drive 9½ miles, crossing over Box Creek. Past the creek, take the first dirt road to the left. A sign just up this dirt road announces, "Turpin Meadows Summer Home Area." This dirt road forms a loop among the summer homes with the other end emerging at the Turpin Meadows Trailhead (see Trails 11 and 11a). The trail begins at the head of the loop, where it is an obvious track up the hillside. There is space to park two cars, but the Forest Service would appreciate it if you would park at the Turpin Meadows trailhead instead. This is about a quarter mile to the south.

Although this trail is obvious for most of its distance, it is not maintained by the Forest Service, and as of 1980 it was completely devoid of signs even at critical junctions. The Forest Service calls it the "Clear Creek Trail," but the Rosies Ridge topographic map labels it the "Turner Cut-off." The Turners once owned the Turpin Meadows Ranch. At the present, Don Turner uses the trail to take hunters to

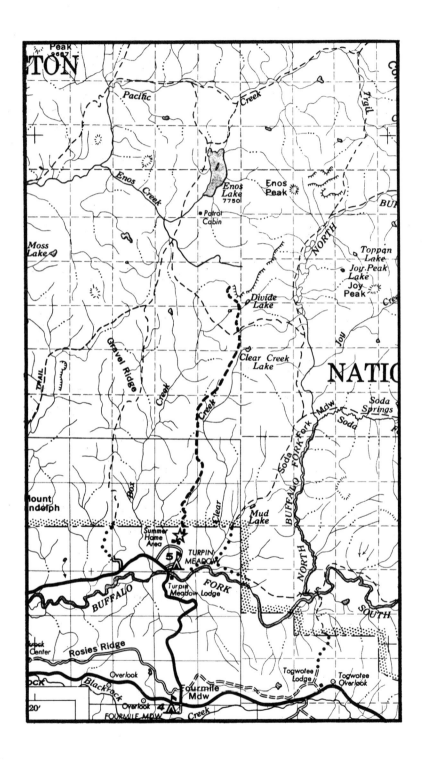

North Fork (of Buffalo) Meadows.

his camp at Enos Lake. You should note that only the Rosies Ridge quadrangle map shows this trail. The bulk of the trail is on other quadrangles, **and they do not show it.**

The Clear Creek Trail starts out very much like both the Lava Creek (Number 8) and the Enos Lake (Number 9) trails. This means a rousing 800 foot climb out of the Buffalo River Valley through aspen, then pine and fir. As you ascend, you are rewarded with some views of the Tetons, the Buffalo Valley, and the Mt. Leidy Highlands to the south beyond the Buffalo Valley.

After a mile or two, the grade flattens out and after a walk through some dense forest where the trail is sometimes very muddy, you enter a large meadow. On the east side of the meadow, Clear Creek flows, exiting at the meadow's south end where a canyon begins.

In July this meadow is a vast field of flowers. The only blight in the picture is the clearcuts visible to the south in the former wildland in the Mt. Leidy Highlands.

It's about a mile across the meadow. Near the upper end, the soil is usually quite damp. The track may disappear briefly, but you should have little trouble finding it again before it enters the forest. One June in this meadow we saw a very large number of bear diggings. I might add that there are quite a few good places to camp in the vicinity of the meadow.

95

At the north end of the meadow, the trail passes into the forest. Soon you encounter a tiny creek (which may be dry by the end of the Summer). You cross this creek twice in fairly quick succession. This is an important place to note because the trail forks here. The left fork (Trail Number 10a) cuts along the ridge side to join the Divide Creek Trail (Number 10b). The more scenic right fork climbs to the ridgetop, giving access to Clear Creek and Divide Lakes, although both lakes are a little way off the trail.

If you want to cut to Clear Creek Lake, walk along the grassy ridgetop admiring the view of the Tetons—also the canyon of Box Creek, odd Gravel Mountain to the southwest, and the Absarokas creeping over the skyline to the east. Descend eastward into the headwaters of Clear Creek and follow it to its source. This is a nice little lake set in a grassy swale with a forested ridge to the east, but with gentle slopes on the south and west suitable for campsites. There is a nice grove of spruce at the southwest corner where most folks camp. Early in the year it can be kind of mushy around most of the lake. The lake has some nice-sized trout, but they are hard to catch.

If you take a few minutes to climb the forested ridge to the east or northeast of the lake, you are rewarded with a beautiful view of the meadows of the North Fork of the Buffalo River, lying far below. The mighty Absaroka Range rises to the east.

Back on the trail, you eventually pass a faint trail leading to the north end of Clear Creek Lake (the long way to the lake unless you are coming up Trail 10b out of the North Fork of the Buffalo). Just past this point, you cross the faint (and unsigned) Divide Creek Trail (Number 10b). Don't miss it, if you want to go to Enos Lake. This is an especially troublesome junction because the Gravel Mountain quadrangle shows Trail 10b going down the wrong drainage (it leads you to follow a drainage too far to the north)!

The next trail you cross goes to the right. This is only a short distance past the Divide Creek Trail crossing. This trail leads to Divide Lake, smaller than Clear Creek Lake, but full of nice-sized trout.

Divide Lake is surrounded on three sides by low, but steep hills. There is a gently sloping meadow on its west side. This isn't generally a good camping area due to ground moisture, but there is a beautiful campsite on top of the hill, just east of the lake. The site overlooks the tranquil North Fork (of the Buffalo) Meadows which lie 900 feet below.

The trail continues northward past Divide Lake, climbs about 120 feet over a meadowy divide (elev. 8800 feet), and descends into the headwaters of an unnamed creek (latitude 57'30" on the topographic map). Here the trail fades out. The Gravel Mountain quadrangle shows the Divide Creek Trail going down this creek. The Joy Peak quadrangle shows no trail. The Joy Peak map is the accurate one. Nevertheless, you can descend the creek to the meadow south of Enos Lake. It is a mild bushwhack. In fact, by keeping to the top of the ridge for a mile farther north and then descending to the west, there are many lovely cross country routes to Enos Lake that ramble through spruce-fir forest and across many meadows that provide wilderness scenes of the surrounding mountains.

10b   DIVIDE CREEK

Length: 6 miles.
Effort: 8 miles either way.
Trail condition: Poor.
Trail use: Very light.
Topographic Quadrangles: Joy Peak, Gravel
    Mountain.

    This is a faint trail leading from the top of the North Fork meadows to Enos Creek, or vice-versa. In between it climbs 1000 feet over a grass and meadow ridgetop that offers fine views of the surrounding country.

    The location of the Divide Creek Trail is not accurate on **any** of the existing topographic quadrangles. The location is correct on the basic Teton Wilderness recreation map, but I wouldn't take the trail without bringing the topos and a compass too. Fortunately, the beginning of the trail is marked by signs at both of its ends. Most confusion occurs near its intersection with the Clear Creek Trail (Number 10).

    Let's begin at the trail's east end and take it to its west end just below Enos Lake. The beginning is at a faint sign just north of the divide between Soda Fork Meadows and the North Fork Meadows where it leaves Trail Number 11a (the North Buffalo-Two Ocean Trail).

    The pathway is faint. The trail climbs through timber and open slopes that offer fine views, to the ridgetop that runs north and south between the North Fork of the Buffalo River and Enos Lake. The trail's crossing of the ridgetop is about mid-way between Divide Lake (which is to the trail's north) and Clear Creek Lake (to its south). Some descriptions (such as Bonney's **Guide to the Wyoming Mountains and Wilderness Areas**), place the trail north of Divide Lake. This is incorrect, although there is an old outfitter's trail there.

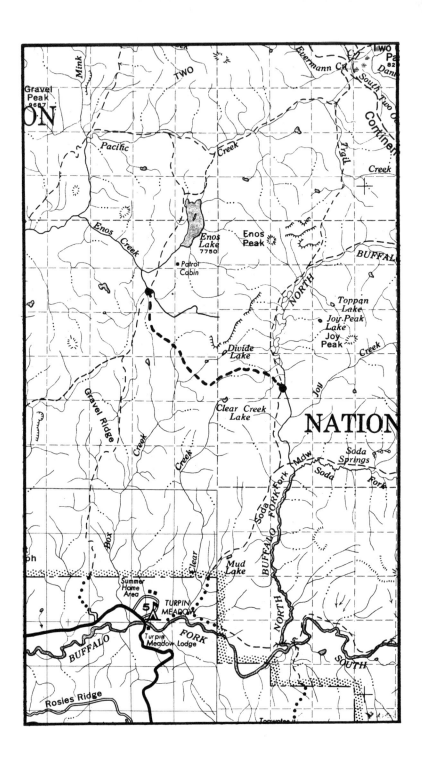

Divide Lake.

You come to an obvious trail just as you emerge from the timber near the ridgetop. This trail is the Clear Creek Trail. Take the Clear Creek Trail southward (this is to your left) for a short distance, and then take the first trail that you come to to the right (west). If you miss it, continue down the Clear Creek Trail for about a mile and take Trail Number 10a, which also leaves the right side of the trail.

After Trail Number 10b leaves the Clear Creek Trail, it wanders about three miles down a series of linear meadows where it follows small streams to its junction with the Enos Lake Trail (Number 9) about a mile below (to the south of) Enos Lake.

11   SOUTH BUFFALO RIVER

Length: 20 miles from Turpin Meadows to
*   Lake Creek.*
Effort: 25 miles.
Trail condition: Fair to good.
River crossings: Five, June 25.
Trail use: Heavy.
Topographic quadrangles: Rosies Ridge,
*   Angle Mountain, Togwotee Pass, Crater*
*   Lake, Ferry Lake.*

The trail up the South Fork of the Buffalo River is a very popular route that leads from the busy Turpin Meadows trailhead 20 miles up to Pendergraft Meadows and Lake Creek.

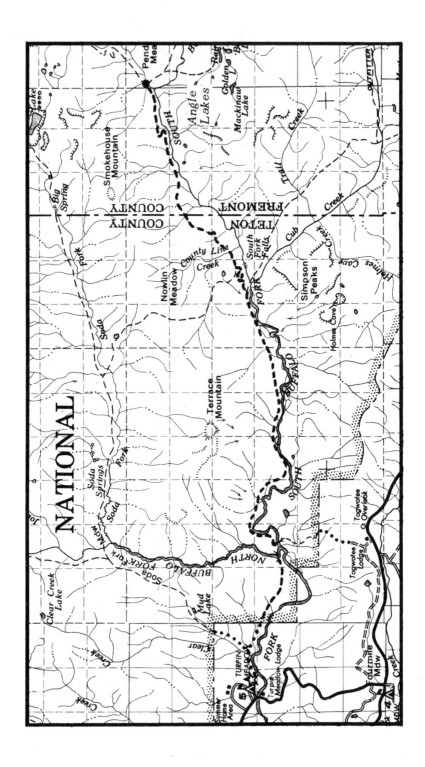

The trail passes through a variety of landscapes near the river and ends near the base of 10,600 foot Pendergraft Peak. From its end, Trail 11c continues up Lake Creek and a seldom-used outfitter trail (Number 11e) takes the hardy hiker to the very head of the South Fork of the Buffalo.

The South Buffalo Trail offers many campsites, good fishing, and the opportunity to see lots of wildlife, especially moose. It should be noted that the trail rarely parallels the river itself, nor does it cross it. Generally, the trail is about a quarter mile from the river. This makes the trail a little bit less interesting than if it followed the river. It also keeps the river's close proximity quite wild, however.

The various side streams can be crossed about June 20–25, allowing a rather deep penetration into the Absarokas for so early in the year. The trail and the meadows will be quite damp, however, that early.

To get to Turpin Meadows, take the Buffalo Valley Road and then drive ten miles to the end of the pavement. Just before the road crosses the Buffalo River, take the dirt road to the left and then take the first dirt road to the right. There are a number of primitive campsites at Turpin Meadows, but no water except the river.

The trailhead is a very busy place. Expect perhaps 20 cars, trucks, and horse trailers. You should note that you can also get to Turpin Meadows by taking a dirt road from U.S. 26/287. This road turns north from the highway 3.6 miles west of Togwotee Lodge and descends 1000 feet in four miles or so. Turn right just after crossing the Buffalo River to reach the Turpin Meadows Trailhead.

There is a trail register right at the trailhead. From here the trail climbs a steep fifty feet up the hill and enters the mouth of the Buffalo River Canyon. For a half-mile (until you reach the Clear Creek crossing), the trail stays about 40 to 100 feet above the river. Here there are some fine views of the Buffalo River, which fills the narrow forested canyon nearly from wall-to-wall.

Clear Creek is only a small stream (no problem except very early in the year). Just on the other side of Clear Creek, the trail splits. The heavily-used Two Ocean-North Buffalo Trail (Number 11a) leaves to the left.

The South Buffalo Trail climbs steeply 350 feet to a forested plateau above the river. There are a couple views of the wild Buffalo coursing through the narrow, 400 foot deep canyon below.

After a brief walk on this plateau, climb 300 feet more across a ridgetop and then drop 500 feet to the bridge over the North Fork of the Buffalo River. A quarter mile downstream from the bridge the two forks blend their waters to create the Buffalo River.

Shortly after the trail crosses the bridge, the Angles Trail (Number 17) joins from the right (the south). The next mile is spent in a rather uneventful walk through lodgepole pine on a bench which is

Pendergraft Peak from Pendergraft Meadows.

about an eighth of a mile from the South Buffalo River. If you hike to the river, you'll find it churning through a minor gorge. The bench ends when you cross a tiny stream. There is a place to camp here. From this point you can see Angle Mountain (10,566 feet) rising to form the south wall of the canyon.

The canyon narrows, and you walk briefly along the river. Many raspberry and thimbleberry plants line the trail, offering a treat in mid-August. The trail leaves the riverside and climbs 175 feet over a pass and then back down to the stream which surges through a rugged canyon. Here is a rock gorge, very dissimilar to the volcanic canyons further east and the soft sedimentary gorges of the western half of the Teton Wilderness. The South Buffalo River has eaten its way down to the bedrock that lies under the Absaroka Mountains, showing that they are not entirely volcanic. The thousands of feet of lava, tuff, and ashflows millions of years ago covered a preexisting mountain range.

You don't stay by the river long. The trail climbs 150 feet over another pass in order to avoid the gorge. Slowly descend from this pass to a lush riverside forest as the canyon broadens. Gradually you approach the river, flowing much more gently now. Terrace Mountain rises on the trail's side of the canyon. Angle Mountain rises on the other.

After passing through a small meadow and a patch of forest you enter Terrace Meadows. Terrace Meadows is about a mile long and half as wide. North of the meadow, Terrace Mountain rises terrace-like (hence the name). The cliff to the south is made of limestone. Above the cliff and a ways to the south is Holmes Cave, an underground recess of some dimension.

Beginning at Terrace Meadows, I've always found that the amount of wildlife seen seems to increase. Moose, particularly, but also elk and deer abound. Fishing seems to deteriorate at Terrace

Terrace Meadows on the South Fork of the Buffalo.

Terrace Meadows on the South Fork of the Buffalo.

Meadows, however. There are some good-sized trout above, but in numerous trips I've found them less abundant than further downstream.

You enter the forest and in a half mile; the Cub Creek Trail (Number 12a) leaves to the right. If you're heading up Cub Creek, you have to ford the South Fork of the Buffalo. Note that the ford is a lot easier in the afternoon than in the morning. You will be painfully surprised at the temperature drop in the river during the night.

After you pass the Cub Creek Trail, you are greeted with a sharp climb of 250 feet. The purpose is to avoid yet another gorge—a very scenic gorge as it turns out. Down in the gorge limestone has compressed the river into a very narrow channel. Midway up, it narrows to a chasm. Here the entire river is seen to plunge through a six-foot wide slot and fall 80 feet over a precipice—South Fork Falls.

You can reach the falls from an easy side trail halfway between the Cub Creek Trail junction and County Line Creek, but for a more scenic route follow game trails from the confluence of Cub Creek along the lip of the gorge upstream directly to the falls.

Back on the main trail, you see a sign denoting the exit of the faint Nowlin Cut-off Trail (Number 11f) just after making the 250 foot climb. In about a third of a mile of gentle ups and downs, you reach the side trail to South Fork Falls. Another quarter mile brings you to the tumbling waters of County Line Creek. Here there is a bridge.

For about a mile either side of County Line Creek, it seems to be particularly excellent moose country. In the three times I've been through, I've always seen at least two moose. Often it is a surprise, with the moose suddenly tromping out of the timber with a snort.

Just beyond County Line Creek lies a mile of mostly climbing up and down through the forest. Here the wilderness changes. You leave behind the aspen. Conifers alone comprise the forests ahead. You also enter the land of the Absaroka volcanics. The cliffs of limestone on the mountains are replaced by walls of dark volcanic breccia with the texture of broken concrete.

The ups-and-downs on the trail end, and you cross the edge of a nice meadow. Here, as you look southward across the river, you see a beautiful mountain wall towering over the dense forest. This is the beginning of the Angle Lakes country. Twenty or thirty small lakes and four large ones are hidden in the timber from here on eastward for about five miles. Many of them are excellent fishing. You reach these lakes by means of a maze of obscure trails that exit southward at Pendergraft and Upper Pendergraft Meadows several miles upstream.

On the opposite side of the meadow you re-enter the forest. It's a mile through the forest to the next meadow. Meanwhile, the trail crosses two creeks, the first having eroded away the trail for a short distance as its waters tumble from Smokehouse Mountain, which is an outlier of the Buffalo Plateau.

While the next meadow crossed is brief, you get a good view of a cliff-like mountain that has been looming closer and closer since your first glimpse of it at Terrace Meadows. This mighty wall is Pendergraft Peak, but curiously enough it isn't really a peak, instead it is the snout of the Buffalo Plateau. If you were to stand on its top, there would be miles of rolling tundra to your back and a 1200 foot vertical drop right before you.

The remainder of the trail is rather uneventful, except for watching Pendergraft Peak grow in size. The trail goes through some open patches and a rundown forest. Then it crosses a marshy meadow with an outfitter's camp near the cliff on its north side. A sign incorrectly labels the meadow "Upper Pendergraft Meadow." In reality, Upper Pendergraft Meadow is about two linear miles upstream and reached by Trail Number 11e, the South Buffalo Outfitter Trail. The various meadows below are collectively referred to as the Pendergraft Meadows.

The trail ends at a fork in a meadow below Pendergraft Peak. Here Lake Creek runs past about 50 yards in the distance. At the junction, a sign says that it's 12½ miles to the Yellowstone River and 7 miles to Ferry Lake via the trail's left fork on what it calls the "S. Fork Trail" (by this, it means the South Fork of the Shoshone River over in the Washakie Wilderness, not the South Fork of the Buffalo which you have been following). The right fork at this junction is the start of the South Buffalo Outfitter's Trail. It immediately crosses Lake Creek and is seen to head directly toward the forest lying at the base of Pendergraft Peak. Hereabouts there are many places to camp.

11a TWO OCEAN-NORTH BUFFALO

Length: 16 miles.
Effort: 19½ miles.
Trail condition: Good.
River crossings: None.
Trail use: Heavy.
Topographic Quadrangles: Angle Mountain,
    Joy Peak, Two Ocean Pass.

This is a highly scenic and well-maintained trail leading up the North Fork of the Buffalo River, over Trail Creek Divide, and ending at Two Ocean Pass, where it joins Trail Number 4, the Atlantic-Pacific Creek Trail.

It is the major route to popular Yellowstone Meadows, due to the scenery and the fact that it is the fastest route to the Meadows. These factors also make it the busiest trail in the Teton Wilderness, and those seeking solitude should take note. It is commonplace to pass eight or ten horse parties a day and several parties of backpackers. Despite the business on the trail, the lovely meadows that

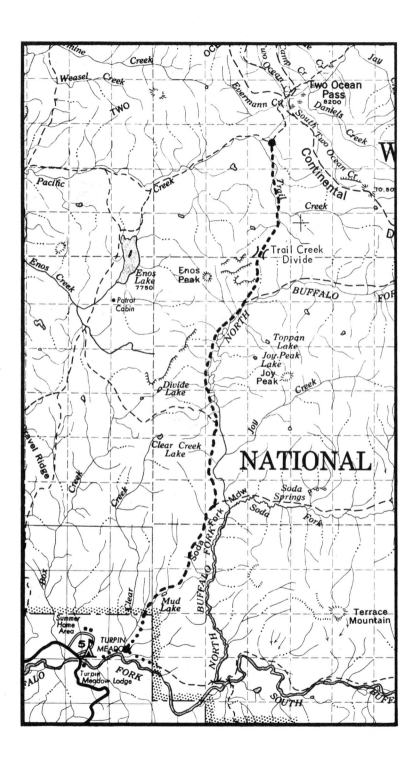

abut the trail are not used much despite their desirability as camp-sites because almost all of the trail traffic is through traffic—on the way to somewhere else.

The trail begins in the Buffalo River Canyon at the crossing of Clear Creek, just ⅓ mile from the Turpin Meadows trailhead. From the trail junction, you climb moderately for 550 feet through small open places and aspen and conifer forest. After 2⅓ miles, the climb ends at a wet meadow called Mud Lake (south side of the trail).

You descend briefly through tall and thick willow brush and then deep forest to break out into a lovely meadow—Soda Fork Meadows.

The southern end of Soda Fork Meadows along the heavily used North Buffalo Trail.

Throughout mid-Summer these meadows are covered with wild-flowers. The mountains you see to the east and the northeast are the Absarokas. The North Fork of the Buffalo, which you will find tracing its way slowly through the meadow ½ mile to the east, forms the boundary between the Absaroka Range and the Pinyon Peak high-lands to the west. The Soda Fork Meadows are about two miles long and are broken up by patches of forest. The trail keeps to the meadow's west side.

108

Northern end of the Soda Fork Meadows near the North Buffalo Trail.

Midway through the meadows, an obvious path leaves the main trail to the right (northeast). A sign here says, appropriately, "trail." This is a short cut over to the Soda Fork Trail (Number 11b), and I recommend it instead of taking the Soda Fork Trail at its "official" start, about a mile farther north at the top of the Soda Fork Meadows. If your goal is Trail 11b, the short cut saves you time.

As you continue up the meadows, a large canyon comes into view toward the east. This is the Soda Fork Canyon. The prominent peak you can see up-canyon is part of Smokehouse Mountain (elevation 10,564 feet).

As you near the end of the meadows, they narrow to form a canyon and you pass two more trails leaving to the east up the Soda Fork. One has a sign. This is the official start of the Soda Fork Trail.

The North Buffalo-Two Ocean Trail avoids the canyon by climbing about 400 feet over a pass and then drops into an especially pretty meadow called the North Fork Meadow.

The gorge the trail avoids is quite interesting and scenic and merits your exploration. Here the North Fork of the Buffalo has cut down into precambrian granite, probably the only exposure of this hard basement rock in the entire Wilderness area. Just as you begin the descent, the Divide Creek Trail (Number 10b) leaves obscurely to your left. There is a sign.

The North Fork Meadow is wider and longer than Soda Fork

Meadows. It has fewer groves of trees and more moose and water-fowl habitat. The peak you see to the northwest is Enos Peak (9522 feet). It is not named on the Joy Peak Topographic Quadrangle. The peak to the right (east) is Joy Peak (10,041 feet). It looks fairly impressive from the meadows, but it is really only a stub on the edge of mighty Soda Mountain which lies out of sight to the east.

About halfway up the meadow, you pass a trail leaving to the left. This is the former route of the Divide Creek Trail. It goes over the ridge to the west and to the south shore of Enos Lake. It is not Forest Service maintained. It is used occasionally, mostly by outfitters.

About ¾ of the way up the meadow, the trail goes through several patches of timber on the extreme western side of the meadow. It then drops down near the river. Here the trail is often wet. You slop through mud as ducks swim on the meadow ponds to the side.

As the meadow is about to end, the trail climbs 80 feet up the hillside. In another half mile you come to a fork in the trail. The North Buffalo-Two Ocean Trail is the left fork; the right is a lightly used trail to the headwaters of the north Buffalo River (Number 11g). The right fork leads past many waterfalls into very dramatic scenery.

Trail 11a, however, begins a climb of almost 800 feet at the fork. The climb to Trail Creek Divide is moderately steep, but on top you are greeted by a gently-sloping grassy meadow that rolls down the other side of the pass and a fine view of Soda Mountain to the southeast. Just as Joy Peak is only a lump on Soda Mountain, so Soda Mountain is

The Teton Wilderness is essential grizzly bear habitat.

but an extension of the massive Buffalo Plateau which lies farther to the east. The mountain you see in the north is the Two Ocean Plateau.

The walk down Trail Creek is mostly gently downhill, passing through forests and meadows. It is three miles to the Atlantic-Pacific Trail (Number 4). You cross Trail Creek several times, but all the crossings are easy. About halfway down Trail Creek, there is a pretty little waterfall near the trail. This is not shown on the maps. You join the Atlantic-Pacific Trail in a large meadow just below Two Ocean Pass.

11b SODA FORK

Length: 16 miles.
Effort: 24 miles from Soda Fork Meadows
to the South Fork of the Shoshone
Trail; 17 miles from the South Fork of
the Shoshone Trail to Soda Fork
Meadows.
Trail condition: Good.
River crossings: Two, July 20.
Trail use: Heavy.
Topographic Quadrangles: Joy Peak, Crater
Lake, Ferry Lake.

This trail takes you up the middle of the three canyons of the forks of the Buffalo River, past some interesting springs, major lakes, and joins with the S. Fork (of the Shoshone) Trail which comes out of Lake Creek on top of the massive Buffalo Plateau. People use the Soda Fork trail as an alternate route to Yellowstone Meadows, but the major destination is probably Crater Lake—a deep body of water at the top of the Soda Fork Canyon (elevation 9300 feet). It's very good fishing.

The Soda Fork Trail begins at three different places in Soda Fork Meadows. Since most folks heading up or down the Soda Fork Canyon will be coming from or going to Turpin Meadows, most will prefer to take the beginning nearest to the Turpin Meadows trailhead. This first entrance leaves the broad North Buffalo-Two Ocean Trail (Number 11a) about halfway through the Soda Fork Meadows. A sign points to the obvious, but faint trail, that leaves to the northeast and reads, "trail." If, for some reason, you want to begin the Soda Fork

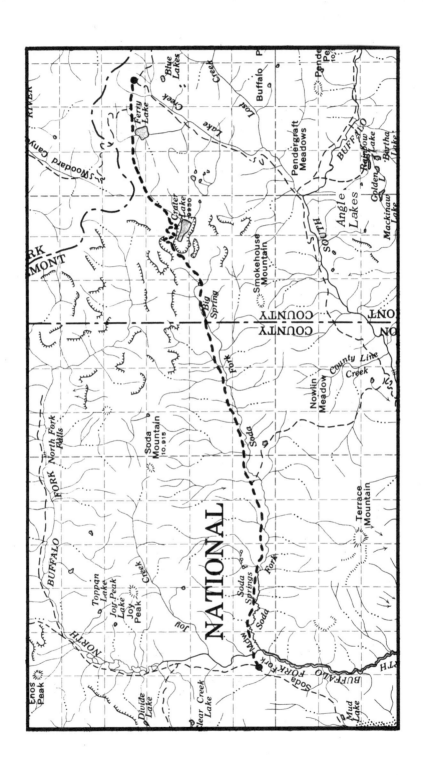

Trail elsewhere, the other two exits from Trail 11a are at the top of the Soda Fork Meadows.

The first exit trail cuts diagonally across the meadows, leading you to the North Fork of the Buffalo River. A trail crosses the North Fork here, but don't take it since it involves an unnecessary ford of the Soda Fork. Instead, follow the riverbank upstream a quarter mile. The trail crosses the North Fork of the Buffalo just above its confluence with Soda Fork. This way you never have to ford the Soda Fork. The crossing is feasible, by the way, about July 15–20.

The Soda Fork of the Buffalo is a bit smaller than the North Fork, but it has a much more constant flow. The North Fork depends on melting snow, but the Soda Fork gets most of its water from Big Springs (a huge spring far up-canyon). Big Springs is believed to be the subterranean outlet of Crater Lake.

Soda Fork Meadows makes a right angle at the mouth of the Soda Fork Canyon. The meadows extend up that broad canyon for about a mile. The trail follows the river closely at first. The stream meanders gracefully through the low willows that fill the lower part of the Soda Fork's canyon. After ½ mile the trail leaves streamside and goes through a more grassy portion of the meadows and right past Soda Springs.

Soda Fork of the Buffalo near its confluence with the North Fork.

View southward from the Continental Divide on the Buffalo Plateau (Ferry Lake in foreground).

Soda Springs are mineral springs (poor drinking water) that are similar to many in Yellowstone, though they are not warm. The view here is dominated by 10,564 foot Smokehouse Mountain. It soars upward from its location about four miles up the canyon. Smokehouse Mountain marks the beginning of the volcanic rock that characterizes the upper portion of the Soda Fork.

At Soda Springs the trail enters timber and climbs gently for perhaps one-half mile. Next, the trail climbs steeply off and on for two miles in a dense forest to the junction with the Nowlin Cut-off Trail (Number 11f).

The forest here is good bear habitat. I've seen several black bears on my trips through. Grizzlies are often seen in the Soda Fork too.

After crossing the tributary stream that parallels the exit of Trail 11f to the right, there is a climb of 200 feet. You pass through an open side slope, around a pond, and enter the Absaroka volcanics. At the open side slope, there is a good view down the canyon that lets you see the colorful rock cliffs on the south side. Soda Fork Canyon is notable for having colored rock in its lower reaches. Almost all other parts of the Teton Wilderness have only white, gray, dark brown, or black rock.

A trek of another mile through the woods brings you to the first of a series of grassy meadows that occupy the middle reaches of the Soda Fork Canyon. This portion of the canyon is truly beautiful. Across the meadows to the north tower the cliffs, peaks, and battlements of massive Soda Mountain. The south side of the canyon presents a similar scene where Smokehouse Mountain thrusts skyward. The best camping sites in the canyon are located in these meadows. To the southside of the meadows, the Soda Fork, still a good-sized stream, runs nearly bank-full the entire Summer. It looks like great fishing, but only small trout are present. Downstream, however, in the meadows of the lower canyon, there are some large trout.

The subalpine beauty of the canyon continues, and in several miles you reach Big Springs. Here the Soda Fork runs full blown out of the hillside amid meadows, patchy timber, and many wildflowers. There is a campsite near the Springs. Due to the beauty of the loca-

Smokehouse Mountain from the lower canyon of the Soda Fork.

Outlet falls of Ferry Lake on the Buffalo Plateau.

tion, it is a bit over-used. Big Springs has a rather steady flow throughout the year, indicating that its source is not snowmelt, but rather Crater Lake which sits 2½ or 3 miles up-canyon (800 feet elevation) above the springs.

You should take note that there is no reliable water above Big Springs until you get to Crater Lake. Past Big Springs the trail begins to climb steeply. You gain about 300 feet, and in a mile pass a small stagnant lake set in a depression with no outlet. Thousands of animal tracks around its shoreline attest to its importance as a source of water.

116

A climb of 350 more feet brings you to Crater Lake. As you climb the remaining mile to Crater Lake, you are rewarded with views of the Tetons as you look back down the canyon. Near Crater Lake the volcanic breccia has been eroded into many odd and grotesque shapes. Don't be surprised if a moose darts out from behind one. Moose are common near Crater Lake.

Crater Lake is fairly large with an irregular shoreline. It is set at the very head of the canyon with its back to the steep slopes that plunge from the top of Buffalo Plateau. Camping is poor on the lakeshore due to steep terrain, but a nearly level meadow to the west of the lake allows camping within a quarter mile. Perhaps the best spot in this meadow is just north of the trail. Here a perennial stream flows. The lake has an island near its southwestern shore which you can sometimes walk to (and camp on) by late Summer. How about the fishing? It is very good for 12 to 16 inch trout. If you have horses, please note that grazing is not permitted within a half mile of the lake. The forage would soon be depleted if grazing were allowed, due to its popularity.

From Crater Lake, you make a breathtaking climb (in more ways than one) to the top of the Buffalo Plateau. You gain 700 feet in just one-half mile. There are unimpaired views of the Tetons, Crater Lake,

Crater Lake from the Soda Fork Trail.

117

Down the Soda Fork of the Buffalo from Soda Mountain.

Soda Mountain, and Smokehouse Mountain. It becomes obvious that the latter two are not really mountains at all. They are only arms of the Buffalo Plateau, extending at a 45 degree angle from one another with the canyon of the Soda Fork between them.

The trail stops climbing at 10,150 feet. You find yourself above timberline, facing a vast rolling landscape. This is the Buffalo Plateau—a mighty geologic feature perhaps fifty square miles in extent, with a very irregular shape, and a myriad of little known wilderness scenes. You can walk for days exploring this land of small lakes, alpine tundra, stunted forests, cliffs, and distant views. You can also get lost—a real problem since you can't descend from the plateau just anywhere because most of it is ringed with vertical cliffs made of rotten volcanic rock. It is silly to wander off the trail up here (or even on it) without topographic maps and maybe a compass. While you may bask in the bright 10,000 foot elevation sun for several days, you may also be hit by sudden severe storms—high winds, hail and snow, and lightning.

Once on top, the trail descends and then climbs again for a mile amid many wildflowers (and mushy ground early in the year). A modest cliff parallels the trail to the north. Finally, you come over a rise (there's a pond just by the trail here on the south side) and get your first view of Ferry Lake—a gem containing very hard to catch golden trout.

Ferry Lake is a mile away from the place you first glimpse it. The trail drops down 300 feet (to 9930 feet elevation) and passes the lake on its north side. Midway to the lake, a trail leaves to the left. This is the first of two spurs to Trail 16. The spur climbs directly to Woodard Pass (10,315 feet) on the Continental Divide. This trail, while direct, is rather mushy and sports a large snowbank at the top until about August. This makes it tough on horse traffic heading for the pass. If you continue a quarter mile past Ferry Lake, a second spur leaves for Woodard Pass. This spur is clear of snow earlier than the first. It is also a bit longer, but more scenic.

Camping is rather poor at Ferry Lake. There are few level spots that are not damp. The best location is at the lake's outlet (south side). There is dry, level ground with room for perhaps two tents here next to a clump of fir right at timberline. Please use a gas stove if you camp here rather than taking wood and defacing these struggling trees.

The outlet of Ferry Lake is spectacular. Immediately, the outlet stream plunges over a small waterfall, then another, and another. Each is greater than the one before. The stream drops off the plateau to join Lake Creek at Lake Fork Falls a mile away and 800 feet below.

Past Ferry Lake, the Soda Fork Trail climbs about 200 feet and then descends briefly across a tributary of Lake Creek (a beautiful small waterfall here), and in a quarter mile it joins the South Fork of the Shoshone Trail (Number 11c).

There is room for much exploring hereabouts. For example, it is a short but beautiful walk to the headwaters of the Lake Creek tributary with the small waterfall. You climb past a tundra pond and, just over the Continental Divide, you are rewarded with an awe-inspiring view of the forks of the Yellowstone River and a lovely meadow along the South Fork of the Yellowstone below. You stand on the edge of a 1200 foot cliff. Some view!

11c SOUTH FORK OF THE SHOSHONE
(Teton Wilderness portion)

Length: 11 miles.
Effort: 15½ miles from Pendergraft
Meadows to Marston Pass; 11½ miles
from Marston Pass to Pendergraft
Meadows.
Trail condition: Fair to good.
River crossings: One, July 15.
Trail use: Medium from Pendergraft
Meadows to Soda Fork Trail; very light
from Soda Fork Trail to Marston Pass.
Topographic Quadrangles: Ferry Lake,
Younts Peak.

This trail begins in the Pendergraft Meadows just west of Pendergraft Peak at the end of Trail Number 11 (see description of Trail 11). Here a sign indicates that the South Fork of the Shoshone

Down the South Fork of the Yellowstone to its confluence with the North Fork.

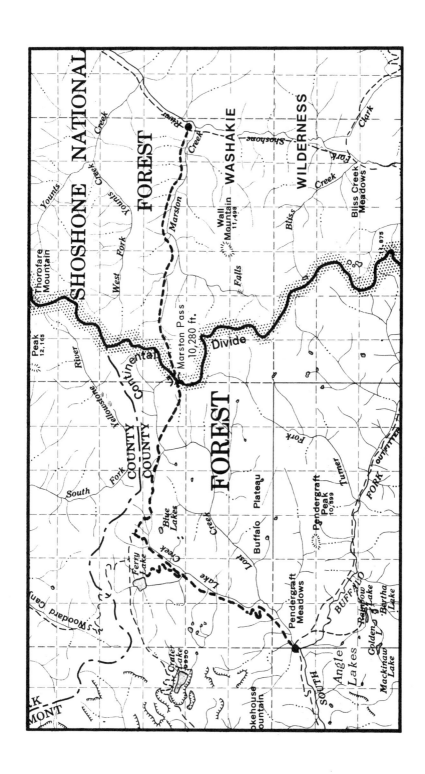

Lake Fork Falls in Lake Creek.

Trail (it says "S. Fork Trail") is the one on the left and the (upper) S. Buffalo River (Outfitter) Trail is the one that crosses Lake Creek after exiting to the right.

It's a long way to the South Fork of the Shoshone River which is in the Washakie Wilderness (about 20 miles). Here, I describe the trail only to Marston Pass, which is the boundary between the Teton and the Washakie Wilderness.

The South Fork of the Shoshone Trail heads northeast toward the walls of the Buffalo Plateau (which tower about 1400 feet overhead). Soon the trail enters the forest and crosses a number of small tributaries of Lake Creek. Then the trail approaches the bank of Lake Creek itself—a good-sized stream. Through the trees you see a large canyon to the right. You may think that this is Lake Creek Canyon, but instead it is Lost Creek Canyon. Lost Creek flows into Lake Creek about a quarter mile upstream from this point (you don't see the confluence from the trail). Curiously, Lost Creek is the larger of the two streams. Lake Creek Canyon, your destination, remains out of sight to your left.

After following Lake Creek for a short distance, the trail makes a steep 600 foot climb up into Lake Creek Canyon. For about a mile there is no water on the trail. Due to the strenuous ascent, you may be wise to carry some water. As you climb, it becomes more obvious that Pendergraft Peak (now to your south) is not a peak. It is the side of a plateau.

The climb ended, you enter Lake Creek Canyon. The lodgepole forest changes to dense fir, and the small open places have flowers, a lush growth of cow parsnip, and other large perennial forbs. A 400-foot high vertical cliff hangs just over your head at the canyon's mouth.

If you walk down to Lake Creek, you are greeted with an awesome sight. Lake Creek suddenly tumbles through a slot in the volcanic rock. The slot is only three feet wide, and the creek's waters plunge into a deep green pool. From here it tumbles into another pool, and then the creek churns out of sight with a roar into a yawning chasm.

Back on the trail, you climb continuously, but at a moderate rate. The lower part of the canyon is narrow and filled with a dark forest. Look for bear. A number of tributaries cascade across the trail providing ample drinking water, but there are few places to camp.

After 1½ miles, the trail switchbacks 200 feet up the canyon slope and for ¾ mile you proceed through meadow and patches of

Toward Marston Pass and the Washakie Wilderness from the Continental Divide.

The Blue Lakes Lobe of the Buffalo Plateau from Point 10,808 on the Continental Divide. Cub Creek Plateau in distance.

forest. Look for moose. Next, the trail descends to a major tributary of Lake Creek (this can be a hard crossing in early July). Just above this crossing beautiful Lake Fork Falls tumbles about 40 feet into a pool. I saw a golden trout swimming in this pool. This is strange when you consider the many waterfalls, rapids, and cascades both above and below Lake Fork Falls. The fish must have survived the trip down from Ferry Lake as fingerling.

Past the falls, the trail switchbacks uphill 200 feet and comes to a fork. The fork to the left (Trail Number 11d) climbs a steep 700 feet to end at Ferry Lake. This fork gets the most use. The fainter main trail, however, continues on up Lake Creek for a mile, then climbs steeply for 200 feet. It then climbs gently for another 120 feet, to join the eastern terminus of the Soda Fork Trail.

Now you are on the rolling near-alpine Buffalo Plateau. The trail strikes eastward, crossing the very top of Lake Creek, climbing a bit, and then slowly descending across many headwater tributaries of Lost Creek. The hill just to your north is the Continental Divide. A short climb from the trail will present you with a tremendous view of the South Fork of Yellowstone's canyon. The headwater streams of Lost Creek keep crossing the trail for the next 3 miles. Water flows over the tundra amid alpine flowers almost everywhere. If you hike off the trail across the Buffalo Plateau, you will find many beautiful small ponds, interesting rock formations, waterfalls, deep canyons, and possibly large herds of elk and some bighorn sheep. You absolutely must carry a topographic map, however, and know how to read it. The Buffalo Plateau is well known as a place where even Teton Wilderness old-timers get turned around.

Shortly after passing above a large wet meadow on the tundra through which Lost Creek runs, the trail begins to climb. You climb about 400 feet in 1½ miles to Marston Pass (elevation 10,280 feet). This is the Continental Divide and the boundary of the immense Washakie Wilderness. The trail continues from the pass, dropping steeply into Marston Creek and reaches the South Fork of the Shoshone River after about nine miles and a descent of 2600 feet. I haven't described this part of the trail.

The view eastward from Marston Pass is tremendous. I rate it second only to Big Game Ridge (see Trail 7d for description) as the best trailside view in the Teton Wilderness. You have to walk just a short way past the pass to gain the full immensity of the scene. Vertical-walled sides of plateaus are visible in all directions. Eroded ridges support pinnacles, battlements, waterfalls, and permanent snowfields. Below, down in Marston Creek and West Fork Creek, the volcanic harshness is softened by green forest. The giant wall to the southeast is appropriately named Wall Mountain (elevation 11,498 feet). This escarpment, an edge of the Buffalo Plateau, drops almost 2400 feet in a near vertical sweep. You are miles from any road and unlikely to meet a soul. I hope you don't gain the pass in a storm. Good luck.

11e SOUTH BUFFALO RIVER OUTFITTER

Length: 11½ miles.
Effort: 16 miles from Lake Creek to head-
waters; 12½ miles from headwaters to
Lake Creek.
Trail condition: Fair to poor.
River crossings: Many, July 25.
Trail use: Light to Upper Pendergraft
Meadows; very light above Upper
Pendergraft Meadows.
Topographic Quadrangles: Ferry Lake,
Dundee Meadows.

The trail to the Pendergraft Meadows up the South Fork of the Buffalo River is heavily used and well maintained, but the trail from there to the South Fork's headwaters is poorly maintained and hard

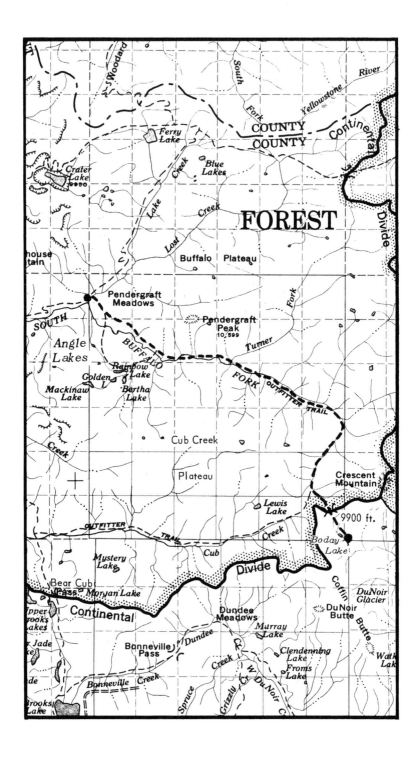

to hike. While the track is easy to follow (except for a short distance above Upper Pendergraft Meadows), it has many unnecessary bends, climbs, and descents.

At Pendergraft Meadows, where the South Buffalo River Trail ends, take the fork to the right (the left is Trail Number 11c), the South Fork of the Shoshone Trail). This outfitter trail heads out across the meadow and very quickly comes to Lake Creek which runs in about three channels. It is a hard ford until at least mid-July.

Continue across the meadow, heading straight toward the wall of Pendergraft Peak (a vertical drop of 1200 feet). At the edge of the meadow, a very faint trail leaves to your right (the south). A sign tells you that this goes to the Angle Lakes (a number of small lakes and four large lakes hidden in the deep forest below the plateau that dominates the southern horizon). Due to the trail's faintness, the deep forest around these lakes, and the maze of trails therein, I don't recommend this route. Instead, take the trail from the outfitter's camp in Upper Pendergraft Meadow if your destination is the Angle Lakes.

At the base of Pendergraft Peak, the South Buffalo Outfitter Trail enters timber, climbs 500 feet over the base of the mountain, and wanders indirectly to Upper Pendergraft Meadow. After about 2½ miles, you enter this meadow by crossing the South Buffalo a little way above where it starts a plunge into another of its short canyons.

Despite the presence of a large outfitter's camp, Upper Pendergraft Meadows is a very wild place. Look for moose. Be wary about a clean camp due to bear (although this isn't the heaviest bear area in the Wilderness).

The trail forks just on the other side of the river. The right fork goes to the outfitter's camp and then up the forested hill to the south to the four big Angle Lakes—Rainbow, Golden, Mackinaw, and Bertha. The first three of these offer excellent fishing. To reach them, cross over the wooden bridge at the outfitter's camp, head uphill, and be sure to take the first trail you encounter. It forks to the left (the south). From the fork it is a steep ¾ mile climb through timber to Rainbow Lake. The other three lakes are nearby, and they are all connected by trails. Camping places are limited, but there are a few camps. Due to lack of forage and space around the lakes, grazing of pack stock is prohibited by the Forest Service.

The trail system continues on past Mackinaw Lake (but doesn't appear on any map) in the form of an outfitter trail used mostly by Joe Detimore. It eventually joins the Cub Creek Trail (Number 12a).

Back in Upper Pendergraft Meadow, Trail 11e (the left fork) heads up the canyon. In places the trail is hard to find and exists on both sides of the South Buffalo River. The several crossings are broad but shallow. The canyon walls begin to tighten, and, after about two

Dundee Meadows with the Continental Divide behind in the controversial proposed DuNoir Wilderness addition.

miles at Turner Fork, the meadow completely ends. From here upstream several miles, the river runs in a narrow canyon. There are no campsites. The Turner Fork side canyon is a sinuous, steep-walled affair with a poor outfitter's trail in it. Its structure is similar to that of both Lost and Lake Creek canyons. All three begin up on the Buffalo Plateau. You may see some bighorn sheep up the Turner Fork, but the most impressive aspect of this area is a beautiful waterfall that tumbles hundreds of feet down the wall of the South Fork Canyon just across from Turner Fork. The wall from which the falls drops is the side of Cub Creek Plateau. The Cub Creek Plateau is about a third of the area of the Buffalo Plateau, and it dominates the landscape between the upper part of the South Buffalo and Cub Creek which lies about four linear miles to the south. Strangely, the plateau isn't named on any official maps.

The trail up the South Buffalo above Turner Fork is not easy. Oh, it's easy to follow, but it climbs and then drops again and again as it zig-zags along the side of the canyon. The trail crosses many small tributaries of the South Buffalo. These are fascinating because they've cut narrow slots in the rough volcanic rock of the Cub Creek Plateau's northern flank. As these snowmelt streams cascade across the trail, the thirsty are rewarded with a cold and delightful tasting drink.

After about two miles, you enter a meadow which is often filled with flowers. This is the last place to camp until the very head of the South Buffalo. The dark walls of the Buffalo and the Cub Creek plateaus rise above you on three sides—a powerful view, especially in mid-summer when the previous Winter's snow cornices hang along the top rims of the plateaus, contrasting with the dark rock.

Past the meadow, the trail climbs steeply (an altitude gain of 300 feet), rising far above the river. Then at this point, the canyon makes a 90 degree turn and heads south. Eventually, you descend back down to the river, which is now much diminished in size. From here to the pass, tributaries and springs seem to run into the river from all directions.

The last half mile to the pass is a broad sloping meadow which is beautiful, but kind of mushy until August. You might see a large herd of elk in this meadow.

At 9900 feet, the pass between the South Buffalo River and Cub Creek is a place of beauty. The view of the Buffalo Plateau as you look back down the South Buffalo from the pass reminds one of famous and much-photographed Squaretop Mountain in the Wind River Mountains. To the west from the pass, a tundra slope rises, providing access to the Cub Creek Plateau. Note that the same precautions apply here to cross country travel as were mentioned concerning hiking off the trail on the Buffalo Plateau.

The grassy turf has grown over the track of the trail right at the divide, but you will have no trouble finding the trail again in upper Cub Creek. Just descend into the canyon on the other side of the pass, and you will soon find it (Trail Number 12c).

There are a few camping spots at the head of the South Buffalo just below the pass, but they are marginal due to moisture and slope. A few more campsites are located at Boday Lake, which is located a mile southeast of the pass.

If you have the time, the short hike to Boday Lake is well worth it. The lake sits in a grassy alpine basin just outside of the Teton Wilderness, but inside of the proposed DuNoir addition to the Washakie Wilderness.

The DuNoir drainage is the last unlogged stream flowing south from the Absaroka Mountains. It is also the last undamaged elk migration route to their winter range. Timber interests in Dubois, Wyoming are trying to alter the situation. A decision on whether to preserve the elk migration path or destroy it for some slow-growing and poor quality timber in DuNoir Creek will probably be made by Congress in 1981 or 1982. If you're interested in saving your tax dollars by preventing tax-funded wilderness destruction by the logging companies, write to your senators and congressmen asking that the

entire DuNoir roadless area in Wyoming be made part of the Washakie Wilderness.

You get to Boday Lake by heading up the small canyon you see just before the South Buffalo-Cub Creek divide as you come hiking out of the South Buffalo. This side trip involves a 200 foot climb over the Continental Divide and then a descent of about 100 feet in the mile to the lake. Here at 10,000 feet you won't be bothered by company.

There are no campsites in the upper two miles of Cub Creek.

11f NOWLIN CUT-OFF

Length: 5½ miles.
Effort: 7½ miles either direction.
Trail condition: Fair to poor.
River crossings: One, July 10.
Trail use: Medium.
Topographic Quadrangles: Crater Lake,
*   Togwotee Pass.*

The canyon of the Soda Fork is separated from the canyon of the South Fork of the Buffalo River by two big mountains—Terrace Mountain and Smokehouse Mountain. Both mountains form impressive barriers to travel between these two forks of the Buffalo. Terrace Mountain is 10,258 feet high. It is composed mostly of sedimentary rocks with many cliffs and terraces between them. Smokehouse Mountain (10,631 feet) is even more rugged, with big walls of rotten volcanic rock—unclimbable in many places. These two mountains do not completely block access between the two canyons, however, for there is a low spot between them (8600 feet elevation). The Nowlin Cut-off Trail takes you through this pass.

One end of the trail is just above Terrace Meadows in the canyon of the South Buffalo. The other end begins at one of the many small tributaries of the Soda Fork in an area of dense forest. For a long time the Soda Fork end of the trail was hard to find, but in 1980 a sign was erected marking the spot. You still could miss it, however. Watch carefully.

Use of both the Soda Fork, South Fork of the Buffalo, and the Nowlin Cut-off trails has been increasing rapidly in recent years, prob-

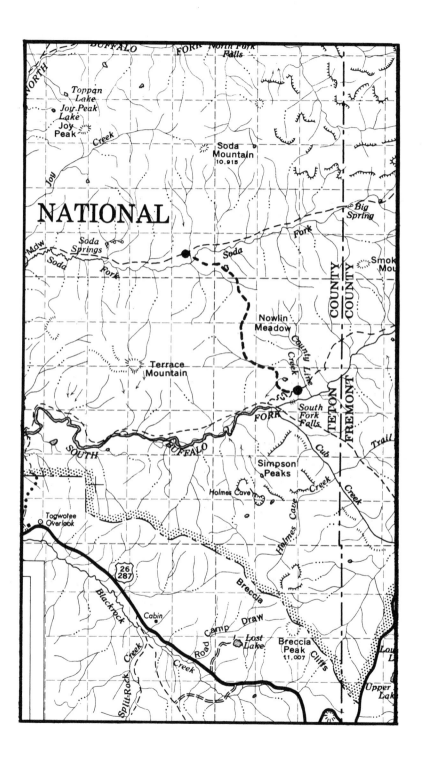

Rain-shrouded Smokehouse Mountain (left) and Terrace Mountain (right) from the Soda Fork. Nowlin Cut-off trail goes through the gap.

ably due to the fact that the three constitute a grand loop. Use of Trail 11f has gone from very light to medium in three years.

Here is a description of Trail 11f from the Soda Fork beginning. The trail leaves the Soda Fork Trail at a small tributary of the Soda Fork. Follow this little stream downhill ¼ mile to a ford of the Soda Fork. On the south side of the stream in a clearing is a Forest Service patrol cabin. Past this cabin climb steeply 300 feet through the forest. The climb ends briefly at a shelf, Here, just off the trail, is a pond. Past this shelf, you quickly resume the climb, and after ¾ mile and another 400 foot ascent, you cross a broad open summit. From just before this summit and beyond the scenery is beautiful, that is if you like flowery meadows and big game.

The damp meadow just on the other side of the summit is Nowlin Meadow. There are often lots of elk here—moose and deer too. You cross the top of the meadow on a slope and then climb briefly through patches of forest and meadow to the edge of another nice and sub-stantial-sized flower field—Upper Nowlin Meadow.

A small stream (a tributary of County Line Creek) flows through Upper Nowlin Meadow. It starts at a pond at the top of the meadow (about ½ mile cross country hike from the trail). In the vicinity of Upper Nowlin Meadow there are many places to camp and lots of little places to explore. Be sure to be careful, however, as the many openings in the forest look similar to each other. You can get turned around.

The trail keeps to the east side of Upper Nowlin Meadow. It leads to the creek, keeping about 40 feet above it on a side-slope, as the creek's waters leap from the lazy meadow to rush down a hillside 200 feet to another flat. The trail leaves the stream's side here, and you climb about 50 feet to a pass between two hills. From here you drop 500 feet in a mile, broken by several brief flats, to the South Buffalo River Trail (Number 11). There is an occasional good view of the deep gorge of lower Cub Creek (across the South Buffalo's stream valley) and also of the broad Terrace Meadows downstream on the South Buffalo.

11g   (UPPER) NORTH BUFFALO

Length: 11 miles.
Effort: 14½ miles.
Trail condition: Good to fair.
River crossings: Three, July 10.
Trail use: Light to North Fork Falls; very
*   light above North Fork Falls.*
Topographic Quadrangles: Joy Peak, Crater
*   Lake.*

Trail traffic on the Two Ocean-North Buffalo Trail (Number 11a) is pretty heavy, but it doesn't extend up the North Buffalo River past the start of the climb to Trail Creek divide. Trail Number 11g to the

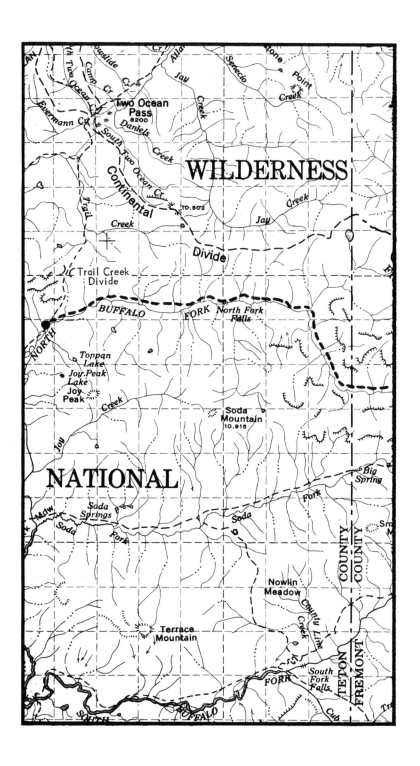

upper reaches of the North Buffalo is seldom used, and yet it is very beautiful, especially above North Fork Falls. The trail is in good condition to North Fork Falls and in fair condition above there. Fishing is good below the Falls, and the camping sites are almost unlimited to the end of the trail. Absence of fish above North Fork Falls probably accounts for the scarcity of people.

The upper reaches of the North Buffalo are notable for their many beautiful falls, cascades, and meadows set between towering plateau walls. Of the three forks of the Buffalo River, I think the North Buffalo has the best scenery.

One half mile above big North Fork Meadows, the many horse parties going to Yellowstone Meadows cut off, climbing to Trail Creek divide. The trail up-canyon immediately diminishes in size, becoming an intimate path, but still easy to follow. Soon the forest openings cease, and you walk through riverside forest most of the way to North Fork Falls (about four miles).

During the first two miles or so, trails occasionally dart off to the left. Don't follow them. Just keep heading up the canyon, which closes tighter around you as you go.

There is one good view before the Falls. Here, after about 2½ miles, the trail steeply climbs 120 feet up a slope to a heavily-forested terrace. From this side slope, you get a good view of Joy Peak's north wall rising to the south above the timbered canyon.

North Fork Falls is a double falls, thundering down through a slot in the volcanic rock. A side trail leads to the falls, while the main trail climbs to a shelf above them. You don't see the falls from the main trail, but on the shelf you get a view down the heavily-forested canyon and your first unimpaired view of the rugged scenery that characterizes the upper canyon of the North Buffalo.

A brief walk through the forest brings you to a large meadow. This is the first of three such meadows between the falls and the top of the canyon. The meadow is ¾ mile long. The trail crosses the North Buffalo twice in the meadow. These crossings are **unnecessary.** Undoubtedly, they developed from horse parties heading to the outfitter's camp you see at timber's edge on the south side of the meadow. Backpackers can use game trails on the north side of the meadow to keep their feet dry.

As you head up the canyon through the meadow, you may think that your trip is about to end. Volcanic cliffs rise to each side and ahead. Is it a box canyon? The answer is no. The North Buffalo makes a sharp turn southward at the base of the walled mountain before you. This "mountain" is actually the Buffalo Plateau, as are the mountains to your side.

At the end of the meadow, you walk for a half mile through forest and openings with many snags from a long forgotten forest fire. The bend southward comes at the crossing of a major tributary

The uppermost meadow of the North Fork of the Buffalo.

of the North Buffalo—Tri-county Creek (unnamed on most maps). This ford can be made after about July 1–10 (depending on how heavy the snowpack was on the plateaus). Tri-county Creek tumbles down a steep, rough canyon without a trail. It has its origin near the Continental Divide in a large, rarely visited lake. This lake is unnamed on the Two Ocean Pass USGS quadrangle, but it is called Tri-county Lake. It's located very near the point where Park, Teton, and Fremont counties shrae a common boundary.

The second of the upper North Buffalo's meadows begins as the canyon bends southward at the Tri-county Creek ford. The meadow is long and sinuous. The trail follows the river closely at times and the trail's tread is just fair (and mushy) in spots. The walls of the Buffalo Plateau rise all about you in massive cliffs, dotted with holes. Camping is good, and very lonesome.

At the end of the second of the big meadows, you're in for a steep climb of 450 feet, all of it through the forest. This is a pity since the canyon walls are at their most impressive height and ruggedness at this point. As the North Buffalo tumbles through this section of the canyon, there is a nice waterfall for those willing to hunt through the forest to find it.

Upon completion of the 450 foot ascent, you stride out into the final of the three meadows. Here the North Buffalo meanders through low willows, grass, and flowers. Looking downstream from about the middle of the meadow, a very impressive wall rises to the left (it's about 700 feet high). While you may not have noticed it, the canyon has made another right angle turn and is now heading eastward again.

The meadow is about a mile long. When you get past it, the trail starts to climb steeply and continuously. The track begins to deteriorate. Don't turn back; the best scenery is yet to come. The very headwaters of the North Buffalo have five or six beautiful waterfalls. You are near timberline where the trail finally peters out, so you don't need one anyway. Just before the end of the trail, one particularly pretty cascade on a tributary leaps just above and below where the trail crosses it.

The trail dies amid a beautiful flowered slope. Cow parsnip, red and yellow monkeyflowers, indian paintbrush, and many other flowers blaze away in July and August, while the North Buffalo's headwaters dash over black volcanic cliffs from their sources on the Continental Divide.

You can find a route from the end of the trail over to the Soda Fork of the Buffalo. Except for a few brief scrambles through rim rock, the route isn't hard, but you certainly should have a topographic map. At times, the flower show on the North Buffalo-Soda Fork Divide is simply incredible.

There appears to be a route over the Continental Divide into Woodard Canyon as well, but I haven't tried it. At any rate, if further rambling on the tundra fields of the Buffalo Plateau isn't in your plans, you couldn't find a better place to spend a day or two watching the snowmelt waters splash and the clouds roll by.

12 BROOKS LAKE ENTRANCE

Length: 5 miles.
Effort: 5½ miles.
Trail condition: Poor to fair.
River crossings: Two, July 4.
Trail use: Heavy to Upper Brooks Lake;
    medium from Bear Cub Pass to Cub
    Creek.
Topographic Quadrangle: Togwotee Pass.

Highest in elevation of all the trailheads to the Teton Wilderness is the Brooks Lake Entrance. Despite the elevation, the trail is almost

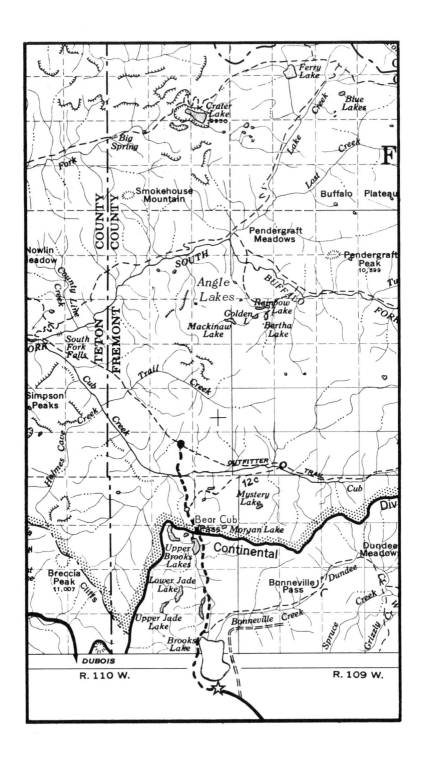

all level or downhill until Cub Creek. The Entrance Trail is surrounded by jagged mountains of great beauty. The big disadvantage of this trailhead is its busyness, not of wilderness-bound travelers, but of auto campers located at the Brooks Lake Campground. Day hikers and campground-tied fishermen have beaten the portions of the trail that pass through damp areas into horrible mudholes.

To get to the trailhead, take the dirt road that leaves U.S. 26/287 23 miles west of Dubois (there's a Forest Service sign). If you're coming from the west, the dirt road is 16½ miles east of Togwotee Lodge. It is five miles on the dirt road to Brooks Lake. Leave your car at the paved parking lot at lakeshore.

Brooks Lake is large, and its elevation is 9050 feet. The lakeside scene is dominated by the towering, jagged battlements of Pinnacle Buttes just east of the lake. They are over 11,000 feet high. To the west of the lake, rise the Breccia Cliffs. Lacking the pinnacles of the mountains to the east, the Breccia Cliffs present a 500–800 foot high wall of regular form all the way from Brooks Lake to Upper Brooks Lake (about 3 miles).

The trail leaves the parking lot and heads around the west side of the lake. Normally, this part of the trail consists of 8 to 10 parallel tracks through a quagmire that used to be a lakeside meadow. The Shoshone National Forest would do well to build a corduroy path around to the north end of the lake, but they probably lack the money. Congress and President Reagan put environmentally-protective appropriations for the Forest Service in last priority (timber cutting funds get top billing from our public servants).

Around the north end of the lake, the condition of the trail improves a bit, unless it's raining (which it often does at this elevation).

Upper Brooks Lake from Bear Cub Pass.

If the trail is wet, the clay soil will stick to your boots in five pound clods.

The trail climbs about 80 feet and passes on the west side of a small, forested hill. Then, the trail descends gradually to a crossing of Brooks Lake Creek. Just before the crossing, the trail splits. The right fork is usually less muddy than the left.

Brooks Lake Creek is full of three to six inch trout of various species. They're hard to catch in the clear, cold, and quiet water.

The trail keeps to the east side of the lengthy, nearly level meadow, all the way from the creek crossing to Upper Brooks Lake. The trail passes the lake through mushy ground and climbs fifty feet to Bear Cub Pass, which is the Teton Wilderness boundary and the Continental Divide.

Upper Brooks Lake is really beautiful, despite the presence of lots of litter. It's mushy around most of the lake, but there is a place to camp on its west side. The lake is full of lots of small trout. Once I spent two days trying to catch one. I didn't. Since then, I haven't bothered to try, even though it may have just been bad luck. Mountain lakes are finicky. In the nearby woods lie Rainbow Lake and a pond.

For a quarter mile past the pass, you follow a narrow, gently downhill-sloping meadow enclosed by forest. A small creek starts in this meadow. Soon, however, the grade of the trail increases sharply. It drops 400 feet in an often-muddy half-mile that runs through deep forest.

You emerge from the forest in a sloping meadow about a half-mile from the ford of Cub Creek. In a big mud-hole at the start of the meadow, there is a fork in the trail. The right fork is the start of Trail 12c, the one you want to take if your destination is upper Cub Creek. If you are heading downstream, keep left. The trail continues to drop and soon crosses Cub Creek. The Togwotee Pass USGS quadrangle shows Trail Number 12c leaving Trail Number 12 very close to Cub Creek, but this is wrong. The trail leaves for upper Cub Creek about a half mile above the crossing, and it follows a route upstream quite different from the south side of Cub Creek Trail shown on the topographic map. Trail 12b, which goes up the north side of Cub Creek is a very poor trail. I don't recommend it.

Trail Number 12 climbs steeply 600 feet after the ford of Cub Creek, and in a half mile it comes to the forks of Trails 12a and 12b. As I said before, I don't recommend Trail 12b (unless you want kind of a cross country hike).

The climb to the trail junction is quite different than the descent from Bear Cub Pass. It passes mostly through sagebrush and aspen. It can be quite hot despite the elevation. There is a nice view to the south of forested Bear Cub Pass, a low spot set between the volcanic mountains on either side.

Cub Creek.

12a (LOWER) CUB CREEK

Length: 4³⁄₄ miles.
Effort: 8¹⁄₂ miles from South Buffalo River
to junction of Trails 12a and 12b; 5
miles from junction of Trails 12a and
12b to the South Buffalo River.
Trail condition: Fair to good.
River crossings: Two, July 15.
Trail use: Light.
Topographic Quadrangle: Togwotee Pass.

I've decided to break the trail up Cub Creek into two sections: the section from the South Buffalo to the junction of the trail coming from Brooks Lake (Number 12); and the section above Trail Number 12 to the top of the canyon. This is because few people make a trip all

141

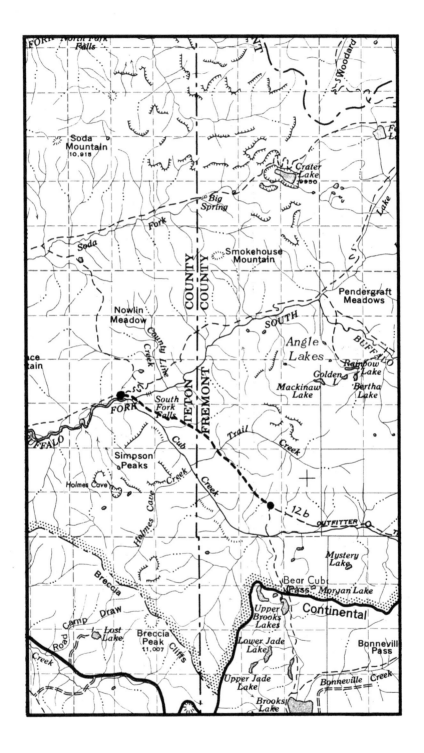

the way from the bottom to the top of the canyon. They either go from Brooks Lake down or up the canyon (most often down the canyon). Alternatively, they come up from the South Buffalo to Brooks Lake, but hardly ever beyond that trail. If you start from the South Buffalo River and head up Cub Creek, you've got a hell of a climb—about 2600 feet to Bear Cub Pass, plus descents adding about 750 feet.

Assuming that you've come from Brooks Lake, the trail begins at the junction of Trails 12 and 12b. Outfitter Trail Number 12b is the faint path to your right (there is no sign).

The trail heads northwestward over rolling terrain. There are patches of spruce-fir forest and many openings. Occasionally you get glimpses of the volcanic walls of the Cub Creek Plateau rising overhead. You are walking along a sub-plateau about 1600 feet below the main one. The rock underfoot is not volcanic. By its white chalky texture you can see it's sedimentary. Cub Creek flows to your left 800 feet down and one-half mile away. You never cross, or even see it on this trip. Interestingly, below where Trail Creek joins it, Cub Creek tumbles through an impassable gorge. This eliminates the migration of fish from the South Buffalo River upstream. Thus, there are few (if any) fish in Cub Creek, even though in the creek's headwater meadows, the habitat looks good.

After walking a mile on this rolling plateau terrace, the trail drops quickly 400 feet to the crossing of Trail Creek. There is a place to camp by the creek—the only camping spot near water on the entire trip to the South Buffalo River.

The climb out of Trail Creek doesn't amount to much. At this point, if you walk cross country to the northwest, you get a fine view of Cub Creek's deep canyon and the Simpson Peaks and Breccia Peak area to the south and southwest.

As you complete the climb out of Trail Creek, a faint trail leaves to the right. A sign says "Trail Creek Outfitter Trail." This trail is not shown on any map I've seen, but it is a shortcut to the Angle Lakes. It might be fun to explore, but it's heavy timber country you could get lost in.

After walking briefly across a forested plateau, the trail begins to descend, at first gradually, and finally, very steeply. For a short distance, you follow a tiny creek (it goes dry in late August). This is the only running water on the trail (except for Trail Creek).

In an open slope about a half mile from the South Buffalo, you get a good view of broad Terrace Meadows on the South Buffalo and the Tetons in the distance.

You can camp on either side of the South Buffalo River. The crossing is about 2–2½ feet deep in August. The fishing is fair. There are a few big trout and some whitefish.

Bear Cub Pass from the Lower Cub Creek trail.

12b (UPPER) CUB CREEK

Length: 7½ miles.
Effort: 10½ miles.
Trail condition: Fair to poor.
River crossings: One, July 4.
Trail use: Very low.
Topographic Quadrangles: Togwotee Pass,
*   Dundee Meadows, with the trail's*
*   location wrong on part of these maps.*

Upper Cub Creek is a pretty lonesome place except during hunting season. There doesn't seem to be any fish in Cub Creek, but there are some nice brook trout in a number of small lakes the trail passes. I was surprised to find that the actual location of this trail on

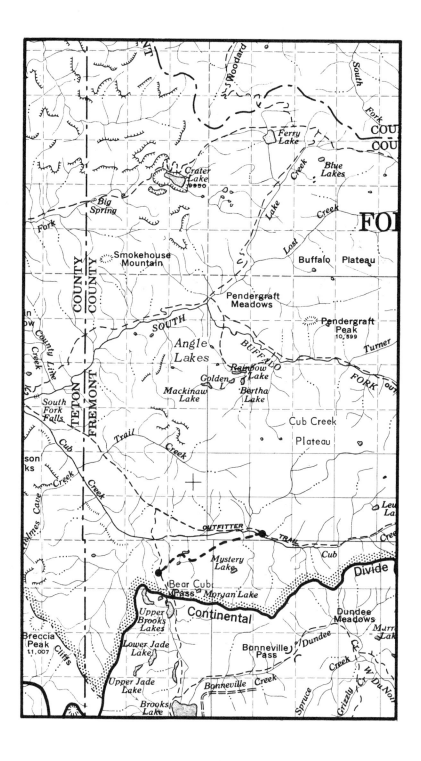

the topographic quadrangles is completely wrong for the first three miles.

The trail leaves the Brooks Lake Entrance Trail. to the right of the mud hole at the top of the first meadow you come to after completing the steep part of the descent from Bear Cub Pass. The trail crosses the top of the meadow and climbs steeply a short distance into the forest. Soon you emerge from the forest and pass the first of several small lakes.

There are a number of ponds and small lakes in the timber here, on and off the trail. You are at the base of a narrow, long plateau which rises to an elevation of over 11,000 feet. The lakes nestled here at its base are very similar to the Angle Lakes that lie at the base of Cub Creek Plateau four miles to the north as the crow flies. The second lake you come to was particularly good fishing when I was last there.

After about 2½ miles, the trail comes down to some meadows next to Cub Creek, and it finally crosses the creek just after you pass an outfitter's camp. On the other side of the creek, you join with obscure Trail Number 12b near where the Dundee Meadows topographic map shows a trail ascending up a side canyon to the Cub Creek Plateau. The trail up this side canyon, by the way, is quite poor.

Before long you drop down a bit and cross a mile-long meadow through which Cub Creek winds gracefully. Here you get some beautiful views of the plateau walls that rise nearly vertical on both sides of the canyon.

At the meadow's end you go into the forest. Very soon you pass a side canyon dropping steeply from the Cub Creek Plateau to your left. Spring-time runoff from this canyon has destroyed the trail for a short distance. Keep going up the canyon and stay on the north (left) side of the creek. You will find the track again.

At an elevation of about 9300 feet, the forest begins to open up and the climb becomes gradually steeper all the way to the divide. The canyon gets narrower, and the nearly vertical canyon walls become lower. The open spaces between the trees are covered with flowers in August. Elk and deer are usually seen near the top of Cub Creek, and I've seen lots of bear sign, including fresh grizzly droppings. After the big meadow, there is no adequate campsite in upper Cub Creek. Once you've passed that meadow you're committed to go to at least the headwaters of the South Buffalo for a campsite by water.

At the 9900 foot high divide, there are beautiful views down both Cub Creek and the South Buffalo Canyon. The divide is broad, level, and grassy. In good weather (it's at timberline), you could camp, but there's no water.

If you want to get back to Brooks Lake, you either go back the way you came, make a long loop via the South Buffalo River and the lower Cub Creek trail, or hike cross country along the plateau forming the south wall of Cub Creek to descend at Dundee Meadows and then over Bonneville Pass to Brooks Lake. This latter hike is really beautiful, but it has some steep places plus some heavily forested, untrailed mountain slopes.

13 THOROFARE-DEER CREEK

Length: From S. Shoshone River to Deer Creek Pass 10 miles; to Thorofare Creek 21 miles; to Bridger Lake 38 miles.

Effort: 47 miles from S. Shoshone River to Bridger Lake; 18 miles to Deer Creek Pass. Alternatively, 43 miles from Bridger Lake to S. Shoshone River; 33 miles from Bridger Lake to Deer Creek Pass.

Trail condition: Good.

River crossings: Numerous, see details.

Trail use: Heavy.

Topographic Quadrangles: Valley, Clouds Home Peak, Thorofare Buttes, Yellow Mountain, Thorofare Plateau, Open Creek, Two Ocean Pass.

The Deer Creek Trail is the only one in the Washakie Wilderness used primarily to get to the Teton Wilderness. Despite the length and steepness of the trail, many people start at the South Fork of the Shoshone River, climb 4000 feet over Deer Creek Pass (10,420 feet) and head right for Thorofare Creek (21 miles). Many go all the way to Bridger Lake (38 miles). It is a hard three days backpack to Bridger Lake; two days on a horse.

While Trail Number 13 is busy, it offers access to many side trails that get little use. This is a very distant part of the Teton Wilderness. If you're heading for this area of the Wilderness (generally called "The Thorofare"), plan to spend at least a week. You'll need at least four days to get into it and back out.

The trail begins near the mouth of Deer Creek on a dirt road 35 miles southwest of Cody, Wyoming. This road up the South Fork of

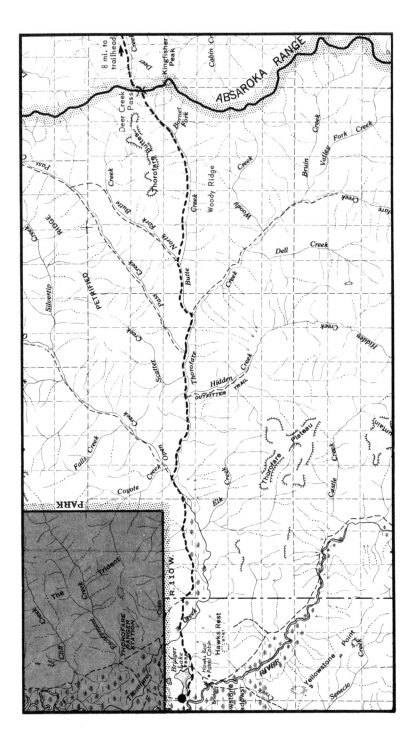

the Shoshone River begins on the west outskirts of Cody. It is paved for about twenty miles. The rest of the way to Deer Creek, it is a good dirt road (though sometimes washboarded). The last 10 miles are a beautiful drive with the Absaroka Mountains rising on both sides of the canyon (some to 12,000 feet), and the broad canyon is dotted with guest ranches. Unfortunately, real estate signs indicate that someday soon it will be filled with recreational subdivisions instead.

The canyon bottom is rather arid. This, coupled with the impressive walls of the mountains, reminds one of the high plateaus of southern Utah.

There's an undeveloped campground at the mouth of Deer Creek. Because there are only a few poor campsites once you start up Deer Creek, it is advisable to camp at the mouth unless it is very early in the day so you can make it all the way over Deer Creek Pass and into upper Butte Creek. Note that this is about 21 effort-miles!

Deer Creek Canyon is a tremendous gorge in its lower portion. The trail keeps high on the canyon wall. It's a beautiful and exciting hike (it's really "exciting" for the dudes that are brought up by outfitters). You should be careful to make way for these parties on horseback. Many horses are easily spooked by backpackers. Keep well to the uphill side of the trail as they pass and don't move around. It's possible that a rider could be thrown from a horse in places on this trail and fall 500 feet into the chasm.

The Deer Creek Trail starts with a very steep switchback climb of 900 feet up the dry, hot face of the mountain (Ishawooa Mesa). Here you have fine views of Carter Mountain across the South Shoshone river valley. Finally, the trail enters the gorge, and often, a cool wind begins to blow. Deer Creek itself churns unseen down in the bowels of the earth, in an awesome chasm to your left. About a mile past the entrance to the gorge, you reach the trail's first reliable drinking water. Here the trail crosses a rock-bottomed tributary that leaps over several waterfalls and into the gorge. Beginning here, and most of the way to upper Deer Creek, you begin to pass many raspberries in August, also currants and baneberries (don't eat the latter).

Past the tributary, the trail climbs higher above the chasm, and then it gradually drops down to the creek and the chasm ends. About a hundred yards above the start of the chasm, you cross Deer Creek (safe, about July 10). Just on the other side, under a dense forest canopy, are a few marginal campsites.

The middle reaches of the canyon (above the lower gorge) give you good views of the high mountains that form the canyon's walls (they rise about 3000 feet very steeply). During part of the Summer, you will see waterfalls on tributary streams. In this part of the canyon, the trail has some rocky, as well as steep sections. While not a bad trail, it is the worst section all the way to Bridger Lake.

A mountain is seen in the middle of the canyon as you continue to

The Trident from Bridger Lake. The vicinity of Bridger Lake is the furthest point from a road as the crow flies in the lower 48 states.

ascend. This is Gobbler's Knob, and it sits astride the forks of Deer Creek. The trail goes up the south fork of Deer Creek (called Deer Creek on the maps). You cross the south fork of Deer Creek and once again climb up a canyon wall as the creek churns through another chasm (although lesser than the one in the lower canyon). There is a marginal campsite just before the crossing of the creek, I might add—poor, but nice to know about for those who can't hike ten miles and climb 4000 feet in one day.

The steepness of the trail finally slackens at the head of the canyon, but this is only a respite to the steep, switchbacking final 700 feet to the pass. The trail is good, but it has steep drop-offs. Before mid-July you should carry an ice axe.

The pass is reached between two gray-walled mountains. The one on the south is named Kingfisher Peak (elevation 11,035 feet). The one you pass directly under is lower and unnamed. The view from the pass is spectacular down both Deer Creek and the other side, Butte Creek. You can see all the way down Deer Creek and to the mountain wall on the other side of the South Shoshone River (Carter Mountain).

Butte Creek, in contrast to the deep V-shaped canyon of Deer Creek, is not nearly as steep or rocky. You can see twenty miles all the way to the Thorofare Plateau, and the view is across the grassy meadows and patches of timber in upper Butte Creek. The most commanding point of the landscape is on the right side of Butte Creek where a mountain with seven steep summits rises dramatically above the canyon's soft greenness. While you can't see all seven summits at any one time, the three or four always in view are impressive. The highest of the Thorofare Buttes rises to over 11,400 feet.

The trail descends steeply for about 500 feet from the pass. The grade then slackens. The trail is essentially a moderate grade downhill all the rest of the way to Thorofare Creek (about 9 miles).

After about two miles, the trail approaches Butte Creek, and there are a few small fish in it this close to its headwaters. The trail then follows a downward sloping bench for about two miles. You pass through a number of small openings and the forest is quite open as well, the result of an old forest fire (notice the snags). You get a number of fine views of the Thorofare Buttes. If you can't get a good picture of them framed by an old burned-out snag, you're a bad photographer. The south side of the canyon (Woody Ridge) is common and doesn't attract your attention.

The trail drops down to the stream's side and crosses it several times (no problem by the time you can get over Deer Creek Pass). After 2 miles or so, you come to the North Fork of Butte Creek, and Trail Number 13b heads up that little-used canyon. There is an outfitter's camp in the mouth of North Butte Creek.

Butte Creek is larger now, and you're not far from Thorofare Creek with its good camping and fishing. In fact, you can begin to catch a few of the big Yellowstone Cutthroat Trout in the creek below the confluence of its North Fork. It's about 1½ miles (with some muddy bogs on the trail) to the trail junction at Thorofare Creek. The trail to the left (Number 13a) crosses the mouth of Butte Creek and heads up into the big meadows of upper Thorofare Creek. The main trail (Number 13) continues downstream, passing through a variety of small meadows and riverside forest. The grade is gentle, and the trail is good except for a steep climb (to avoid crossing Thorofare Creek) just before the confluence of Pass Creek.

Pass Creek isn't difficult to cross, but it's bigger than North Butte Creek. It's filled with medium-sized, round rocks at the crossing. About 200 yards past the crossing, the Pass Creek Trail (Number 14) leaves the Thorofare Trail at a signed junction.

Another 1½ miles brings you to the Hidden Creek Outfitter Trail (Number 13c). This is easy to miss (as of 1977 there was no sign), and though Hidden Creek is a tremendous canyon, its mouth is narrow and obscure. One could walk by it. Anyway, the Hidden Creek Trail is the first trail to the left past Pass Creek. If you miss it, you get another chance. A second spur to Hidden Creek leaves a quarter mile further down Thorofare Creek. Its condition is poor, however—lots of down timber.

Bridger Lake in the rain. View is to the northwest.

It's another 2–2½ miles to Open Creek, the major tributary of Thorofare Creek. This distance to Open Creek consists of a walk through meadows and forest on a bench which keeps about a quarter mile from Thorofare Creek. Open Creek is a good-sized stream, but it can be forded by the time of year you can get over Deer Creek Pass or up from Bridger Lake (which involves a ford of tougher Thorofare Creek). Just prior to the ford you get a partial view of the cliffs that line the edge of the 11,000 + foot Trident Plateau on the northwest side of the Open Creek Canyon.

After the ford, you climb 100 feet up a mountain slope, and here the Open Creek Trail (Number 15) leaves to the right. Below Open Creek, the Thorofare's valley widens, and the creek's margins become marshy, resulting in excellent moose habitat. The trail keeps to the north side of the valley about a half-mile away from the stream itself.

After you go about 3½ miles, the trail forks. The right fork heads into Yellowstone, going first past a Wyoming Game and Fish cabin almost on the Park boundary and then to the Park Service's Thorofare Ranger Station (occupied) ¾ mile north of the Park boundary.

The left fork (Trail Number 13) cuts toward the creek and crosses it in another mile and a half. Thorofare Creek is a big stream. The ford isn't reliable until about July 30 (this, of course, varies by a week or so each year). At the ford, the landmark, Hawks Rest Mountain rises 1200 feet above the timber south of the creek.

A mile and a quarter past the ford, you come to a 4-way junction in a small opening. The trail to the right and the one straight ahead lead to opposite ends of Bridger Lake. The trail to the left leads to the Forest Service's Hawks Rest Patrol Cabin. You can usually find a ranger there.

I've already mentioned the good fishing in Bridger Lake. Thorofare Creek is excellent fishing almost its entire length. It is full of big Yellowstone Cutthroat Trout. They run up the creeks to spawn in early Summer. However, they remain to be caught until about mid-August. In Thorofare Creek they range from about a foot to twenty inches. Many people, and the number is increasing, head for the upper Yellowstone River, Bridger Lake, and the Thorofare to catch these beautiful fish in their wilderness home.

Let me give a few words of caution. The spawning trout in early Summer bring quite a few bears to Thorofare. Of course, it's hard for many people to get in the country that early. You may also notice that as you clean an occasional fish, small worms will crawl out of the flesh. This is no problem at all if you cook the fish properly. However, they are tapeworm larva. They need to be eaten raw by a warm-blooded animal to complete their life-cycle. You are a warm-blooded animal. They can grow twenty feet long in your intestines.

13a UPPER THOROFARE CREEK

Length: 9½ miles.
Effort: 10¾ miles from Butte Creek
  crossing to head of the upper meadow.
Trail condition: Fair.
River crossings: Three, July 10.
Trail use: Heavy.
Topographic Quadrangles: Thorofare
  Plateau, Yellow Mountain.

This is an easy trail, used heavily by fishermen on day trips from

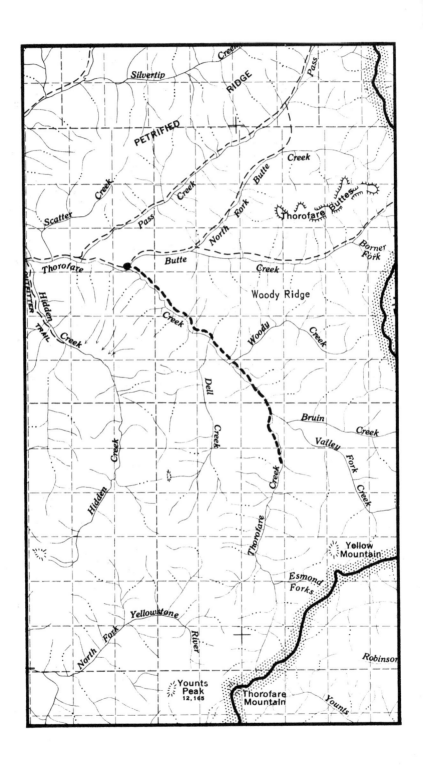

outfitters' camps. It's mostly through big meadows around which rise increasingly big mountains. It is not a through trail, so the traffic decreases as you move up the trail. I'd classify the use as heavy until Valley Creek (sometimes really heavy). In the meadow above Valley Creek, maybe medium is more accurate. You'll find a good portion of the users not on the trail, but down by the river lashing the waters.

Trail 13a leaves Trail 13 at a signed junction. Trail 13a crosses Butte Creek right at its confluence with Thorofare Creek. You should be able to get across Butte Creek here by the time you can get in from Deer Creek Pass or up from Bridger Lake with no trouble.

Even this far upstream, Thorofare Creek is large. The trail follows the stream closely at first, but the trail soon climbs a side slope through forest and quickly drops down to the start of the first meadow. The meadow's lower end is being invaded by lodgepole pine, but as the meadow broadens, the vegetation declines to grass, flowers, low willows, and some sagebrush. Scenery improves as you saunter up this tranquil meadow. The big mountain ahead is Yellow Mountain (over 11,400 feet). The trail keeps to the left side of the meadow. As you walk, you will probably find pieces of petrified wood. You can find it everywhere in the Thorofare country, but it is especially common in Thorofare Creek, North Butte Creek, and Pass Creek.

After about two miles, you pass a narrow canyon that runs in from the right side of the meadow (Dell Creek). Very soon you cross a stream from your side (Woody Creek). From here to the top of the meadow, Thorofare Creek and its tributaries meander a great deal and fill the valley with many stream channels.

Valley Creek crosses the trail at the top of the meadow. You enter forest and climb about 140 feet along the rim of a small canyon of Thorofare Creek to the upper meadow. Here in the upper meadow the trail is poor, and it splits to make a loop around either side. The scenery is very pretty. The walls of the Thorofare Plateau rise above you on the west and southward (ahead). The slopes of Yellow Mountain climb, but not quite so steeply, on the east side of the meadow. Permanent snowfields dot the rim of the plateau ahead and they feed the cascades you can see.

13b NORTH FORK OF BUTTE CREEK

Length: 6½ miles.
Effort: 10 miles from mouth of North Butte
Creek to Pass Creek; 8½ miles from
Pass Creek to mouth of North Butte
Creek.
Trail condition: Poor.
River crossings: Three, easy.
Trail use: Very light.
Topographic Quadrangle: Thorofare Buttes.

This is a scarcely-used trail (except during hunting season) that follows the canyon of North Butte Creek and then crosses into Pass Creek, where it joins the Pass Creek Trail. Trails 13b, 14, and 13 make a nice loop into a remote part of the Thorofare Country for those more interested in the mountains than the fishing. Parts of the trail are hard to find.

Our trail leaves Trail 13 in Butte Creek just west of the North Butte Creek crossing. You can't miss the canyon as there is an outfitter's camp right in its mouth. The trail goes right through the camp (which is unoccupied except during hunting season). On the other side of the camp, the trail splits. Keep to the right. The trail climbs steeply for a hundred feet to a forested bench, but it soon drops back down. After ½ mile (mostly through forest), you cross North Butte Creek. Before long the canyon begins to open up and broaden a bit. After three miles of walking on the narrow and winding trail, you reach the open, flowery head of the canyon. There is only a low ridge to your left, but to your right (the south) the Thorofare Buttes rise. Unfortunately, the view isn't as good as on trail Number 13 at the top of Butte Creek. At the head of the canyon you see a number of fine peaks—all of them unnamed. These peaks are the Absaroka crest and form the boundary between the Teton and Washakie Wildernesses.

At the top of the meadow, two streams come together to form North Butte Creek at the base of a low, forested hillock. The trail crosses here, follows the left fork briefly, and then ascends the low ridge on the north side of the canyon. It is a 600 foot climb to the pass. This is the most scenic part of the hike. To the south, you see the Thorofare Buttes in their full glory. This side looks different than the Butte Creek side. Instead of dropping continuously to the stream bottom, the Buttes here rise above two large cirque basins. Below the basins they plunge for a second time while secondary buttresses stand watch.

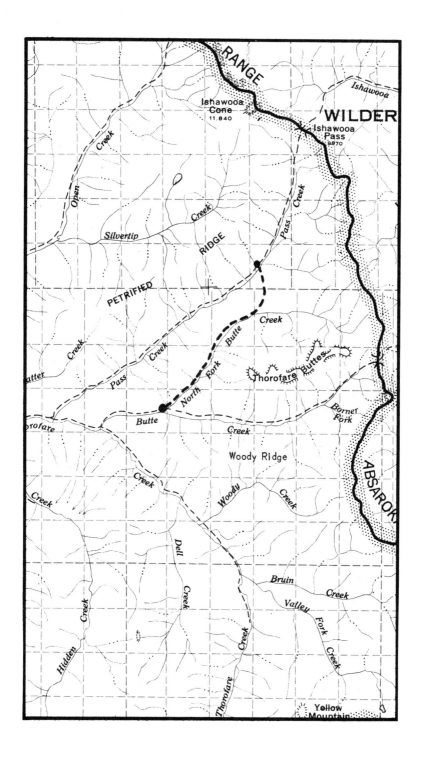

From the pass, the view into upper Pass Creek is extraordinary. Up the left side of the canyon runs rugged Petrified Ridge which grows higher as it approaches the Absaroka crest. At the end of the canyon, the low spot is Ishawooa Pass, providing secondary access to the Teton Wilderness from the Washakie. Below you, the lush Pass Creek meadows extend all the way to canyon's end.

The view ends as you pitch down the north side of the ridge into forest. After dropping 600 feet, you cross a small creek and come out into the Pass Creek meadow. Here at 9000 feet are lovely places to camp. The trail continues upstream for a half mile to join the Pass Creek Trail (Number 14). If you want to go down Pass Creek, the topography offers no barriers to cutting downstream to join Trail 14.

There is lots of petrified wood in North Butte and Pass Creek. You can also find petrified trees. In a spot on the hillside about 300 feet above the outfitter's camp in the mouth of North Butte Creek, I found a perfectly preserved petrified stump five feet high and as much in diameter. Please don't deface these specimens. If you have to carry some out, take one of the many pieces that lie on the ground. Even then, you'll probably find it heavy enough that you'll have to discard it before you walk the fifteen miles plus out of the Wilderness.

13c HIDDEN CREEK OUTFITTER'S

Length: 3 miles.
Effort: 4 miles.
Trail condition: Fair.
River crossings: One, July 20.
Trail use: Medium.
Topographic Quadrangle: Thorofare
  Plateau.

Although the mouth of Hidden Creek is only a narrow slot easily overlooked by passers-by, it is probably the most spectacular canyon in the Teton Wilderness. Once you get past its obscure entrance, its tremendous scenery increases all the way to its head where an icy-cold waterfall plunges off the Thorofare Plateau. Through much of this canyon's length, massive volcanic walls rise 800 to 2000 feet on both sides. Hidden Creek is a good place to find elk, deer, and bear. The Thorofare Plateau that surrounds the canyon is well known for its herd of bighorn sheep.

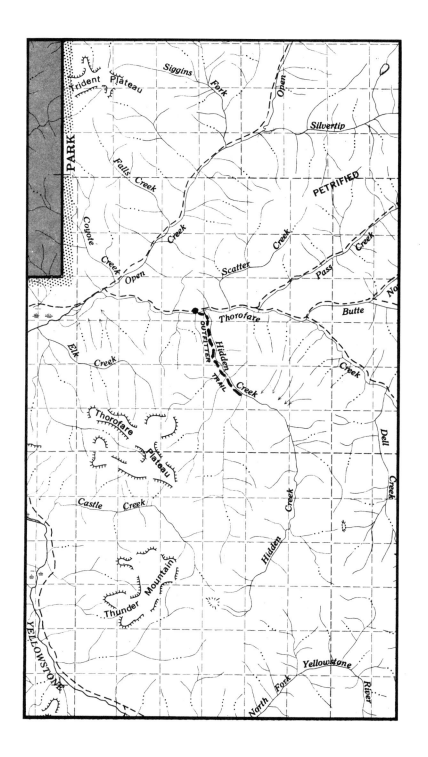

The Thorofare Plateau (highest point, Thunder Mountain) is the highest of the plateaus in the Teton Wilderness. It is also much more rugged than the Buffalo Plateau on top. It rises to 11,797 feet and even has a few small glaciers in some of the north-facing slopes near the plateau's south end.

The Hidden Creek Trail leaves the Thorofare Trail (Number 13) about a mile and a half below Pass Creek and two miles above Open Creek. There are two entrances to this trail about a quarter mile apart. They both exit to the south, but the one that exits the furthest down Thorofare Creek had a lot of downed timber as of 1977. Both exits join at the edge of Thorofare Creek at an abandoned outfitter's camp. You could have a nice camp here.

The Hidden Creek Trail fords Thorofare Creek. This is not an easy wade until August. I guess July 20 is about the earliest it can be done most years, unless you have a horse. On the creek's other side, the trail crosses a wet meadow on a corduroy path. It then makes a brief, but very steep, climb through dense timber. On top, the trail goes through a narrow meadow enveloped by really deep forest on each side. The meadow ends after a third of a mile. Again, the trail makes a very steep climb, gaining about one hundred feet in elevation. Finally, it emerges into the first of many beautiful openings and meadows of Hidden Creek Canyon. You get your first view of the plateau walls surrounding the canyon. The prominent peak ahead is 10,770 feet high and marks the forks of Hidden Creek. The right fork is called "Camp Creek" by wilderness old-timers. Hidden Creek goes to the left of the mountain.

Soon you cross two small creeks in rapid succession. Local outfitters call these First Creek and Second Creek. From here it is ¾ mile to the end of the trail at Camp Creek (named after the outfitter's camp there). From the camp other minor trails radiate. You can follow them or not. It isn't hard to get around in Hidden Creek (unless you try to climb out of it). The meadows increase in beauty as you continue up the canyon, and there are many places to camp by the creek. The creek itself has cutthroat trout up to about ten inches in length. It doesn't participate in the Yellowstone Lake cutthroat spawning runs, however, due to the narrowness of the creek's canyon mouth, so you won't hook a big one.

14 PASS CREEK

Length: 9½ miles.
Effort: 13 miles from mouth of Pass Creek
to Ishawooa Pass.
Trail condition: Fair.
River crossings: None.
Trail use: Low.
Topographic Quadrangles: Thorofare
Plateau, Open Creek, Thorofare Buttes.

This trail leads from Thorofare Creek up a narrow canyon that broadens into a big meadow at its head. From the head it switchbacks over Ishawooa Pass (elev. 9915 feet) and into the Washakie Wilderness. The upper part of the canyon is really pretty and on most days you won't pass a single soul, even though this route is the secondary access from the Washakie Wilderness (Deer Creek being the primary).

Trail Number 14 begins at the mouth of Pass Creek about 100 or 200 feet west of the Pass Creek ford on the Thorofare Creek Trail. You walk through a flat meadow and into a narrow canyon. For the first 2½ miles, the trail keeps quite close to the stream and passes mostly through forest. The scenery is pleasant, but not exciting. Then, for about a mile, you climb on the canyon's side about 100 feet above Pass Creek. When the trail once again meets the creek, you break out into a beautiful meadow that extends all the way to the end of the canyon (about 4½ miles). The ridge on the left side of the canyon with the forested base and meadowy slopes is Petrified Ridge. It gets higher and higher all the way to the pass, culminating in 11,853 foot Ishawooa Cone. As its name indicates, there is a lot of petrified wood on the ridge. The ridge to the right side of the canyon is much less continuous than Petrified Ridge, being broken up by two tributary canyons.

As you near the end of the meadow, you can see Ishawooa Pass as a distinct low spot in the Absaroka crest. A rugged, odd-shaped mountain 10,903 feet high rises to the right of the pass. The higher Ishawooa Cone to the left isn't quite as visible. The climb to the pass from the top of the meadow is only 600 feet, with the last 200 being the only really steep part.

From Ishawooa Pass you have a beautiful view of Wapiti Ridge as you look northeastward across Ishawooa Creek's headwaters. Wapiti Ridge's steep slopes rise over 3000 feet in places from the canyon bottom. The ridge's high point is the appropriately named 11,619

161

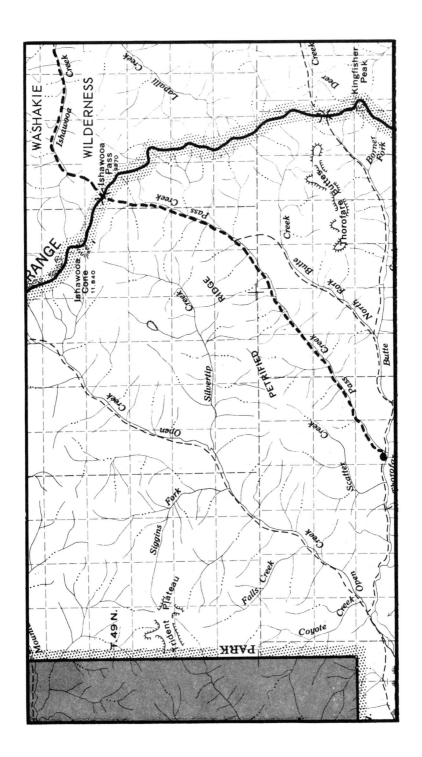

foot Clouds Home Peak. The switchbacking descent into Ishawooa Creek is twice as great as the climb from Pass Creek—1200 feet. The rest of the trip down Ishawooa Creek is beautiful, similar in places to Deer Creek (see the description of Trail Number 13). I haven't described it since it is only a secondary access to the Teton Wilderness and is many miles in length (about 20 miles). Ishawooa Pass is passable on horseback about July 15–20. Ishawooa Creek has bridges to make its crossings easier.

15 OPEN CREEK

**Length: 11 miles to end of trail, 13 miles to
   Rampart Pass.**
**Effort: 13 miles to end of trail; 20 miles to
   Rampart Pass.**
Trail condition: Good to fair.
River crossings: Five easy tributaries.
**Trail use: Medium to Silvertip Creek, very
   light above Silvertip Creek.**
**Topographic Quadrangles: Open Creek,
   Thorofare Buttes, Sheep Mesa.**

Open Creek is the biggest tributary of Thorofare Creek. It is good fishing for big trout in its lower portions. This fact brings a fair number of people upstream for a way, but since there is no real trail through to the Washakie Wilderness (despite what the maps may show), you won't meet people in the upper part of its canyon.

Rugged mountains line the sides of the canyon most of its distance, although you don't get many good views of them until you are well past Silvertip Creek (Open Creek's major tributary).

The name "Open Creek" may imply that the canyon is full of wide open meadows, but this is not so (although it has some near the creek). Perhaps at one time during exploration days there were more meadows (as after a fire). More likely, the name comes from the fact that it is a big canyon—one-half mile wide at its mouth. The trail, however, keeps to the forest for much of the way. The trail's condition is generally pretty good for being a side trail.

The trail begins 1/5 mile before the crossing of Open Creek (for

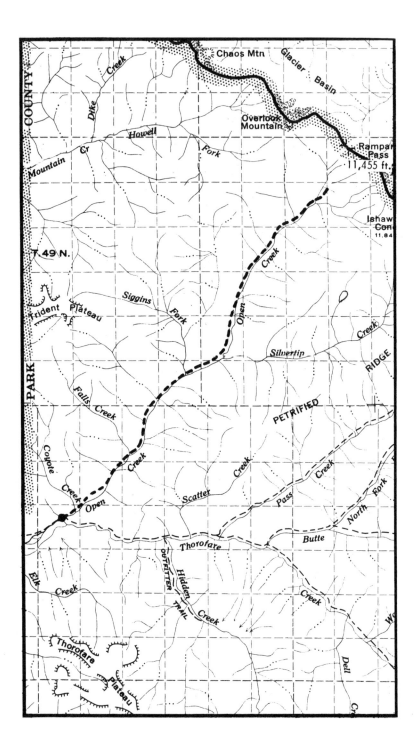

those coming up Thorofare Creek). It begins a little way up a mountain slope in an open spot. The trail drops down about 40 feet, and you walk through forest and cross the first of five tributaries after a third of a mile (this is Coyote Creek). None of the five tributaries are difficult by the time you can get into Open Creek.

It's two miles to the next side creek (Falls Creek). The trail climbs a little bit and then goes down a bit. There are a few views of Petrified Ridge to the southeast (the right side of the canyon) as you cross an occasional open slope. You cross Falls Creek in the forest. The creek has its origin in a permanent snowfield high on the Trident Plateau. This plateau is perhaps the least-known of the plateaus of the Teton Wilderness. It's high (11,123 feet), but not very expansive (unless you want to include the many-peaked ridge that connects it to the Absaroka crest, ending at Overlook Mountain). Falls Creek owes its name to a 200 foot high falls near its top. I haven't been there. It looks like it would be a tough bushwhack.

It's a mile and a half to the next tributary (unnamed). This one also starts at a snowfield on the Trident Plateau and has a waterfalls near the head of its side canyon.

For the next mile, you follow Open Creek more closely and walk through four meadows to the crossing of Siggins Fork, the biggest of the five tributaries that flow into Open Creek from the left side of the canyon.

Soon you will notice a large canyon that comes into Open Creek from the right. This is Silvertip Creek. The Silvertip Creek Outfitter Trail leaves the Open Creek Trail about a mile-and-a-half **above** Silvertip's confluence with Open Creek. The Silvertip Creek Trail (Number 15a) leaves at an outfitter's camp (mostly torn down in the Summer, so look closely).

In the vicinity of this camp, Open Creek starts to become meadowy. The views of the rugged mountains improve. About a mile farther up, you cross what I guess to be tributary 5½ (it's smaller than the rest). Scenic mountains rise on both sides of the trail to over 11,000 feet. You cross the last tributary in a mile. Soon, in lovely meadows near 9000 feet, the trail peters out.

All the maps show a trail over Rampart Pass into the Shoshone National Forest and the Washakie Wilderness, but this trail is only a hiking route (some very experienced horsemen may be able to ride the pass). I haven't been to the pass, but that's what I've heard. Apparently, the route doesn't really go over a pass, but rather directly over the 11,455 foot peak just south of Overlook Mountain! From there it follows a knife-edge ridge with the Fishhawk Glacier 600 feet below on one side and the Rampart Creek Glacier on the other. Then you descend into Rampart Creek and walk twenty miles to the trailhead (or so I'm told).

15a SILVERTIP CREEK OUTFITTER

Length: 7 miles.
Effort: 10 ½ miles from Open Creek to Pass
Creek; 9 miles from Pass Creek to
Open Creek.
Trail condition: Fair to poor.
River crossings: One, July 15.
Trail use: Very low.
Topographic Quadrangles: Open Creek,
Thorofare Buttes.

Here's a trail way back in the Thorofare Country where you'll be completely alone. Probably the only people that go up it are guided hunters in September or October. The trail is not Forest Service maintained, and it's a bit hard to find the start of it at either end. Finding it in Open Creek is easiest. Parts of the trail are beautiful, especially on top of Petrified Ridge where the trail climbs over a 10,250 foot high pass.

The Silvertip Creek Trail begins in Open Creek about 1½ miles **above** Silvertip Creek's confluence with Open Creek. It leaves Open Creek at an outfitter's camp that is largely taken down in the summer and, therefore, a little hard to spot. Outfitter Sam Siggins does a really good job keeping the wilderness environment here clean. He deserves credit. If you're coming up Open Creek and don't want to walk the extra distance above Silvertip Creek in order to begin at the start of the trail, you can cut cross country to the trail, joining it in Silvertip Creek Canyon. The cross-country route is through timber and meadow on a moderate grade.

The trail keeps to the left (north) side of the stream. It passes mostly through forest with few views until you reach the upper part of the canyon. Here there is a meadow where rugged mountains rise on all sides. The peak at the head of the canyon is unnamed and rises to 11,352 feet.

The trail climbs out of the canyon, rising 1300 feet on a rough and rugged trail, to the top of Petrified Ridge at 10,252 feet. On this grassy divide, the trail fades out, but you may find a track heading N.-N.E. along the ridgetop. The outfitter uses this to get to Ishawooa Pass at the head of Pass Creek. This is the wrong trail unless Ishawooa Pass is your destination. Instead, drop N.E.-E. off the divide and you should find a rough trail that switchbacks down Petrified Ridge to the lovely grass and flower meadow of upper Pass Creek.

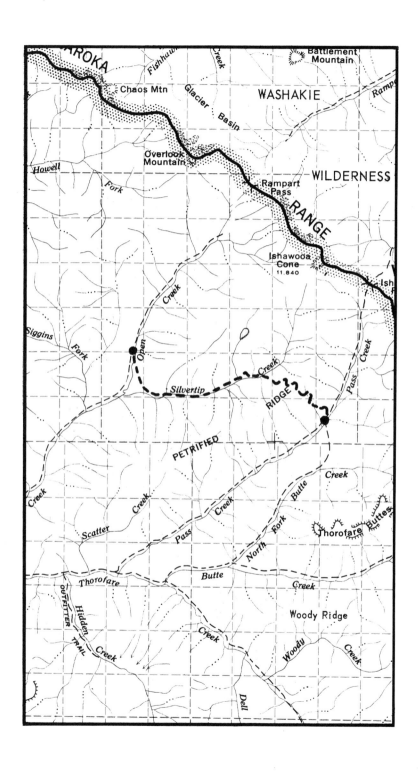

Silvertip Creek isn't for fishing. It's a trip for the scenery in the upper canyon and on the pass. You'll be all alone. A few of the big critters that gave the canyon its name are there still, but not necessarily in a higher concentration than in Open Creek or a number of other places in the Thorofare. You can find plenty of petrified wood on Petrified Ridge.

16 UPPER YELLOWSTONE RIVER

Length: 15½ miles.
Effort: 16 miles from Ferry Lake to Hawk's
  Rest Patrol Cabin; 20½ miles from
  Hawk's Rest Patrol Cabin to Ferry Lake.
Trail condition: Good to fair.
River crossings: One, July 25.
Trail use: Medium.
Topographic Quadrangles: Ferry Lake,
  Thorofare Plateau, Two Ocean Pass.

This trail is a secondary route to the famous Yellowstone Meadows and Bridger Lake. It goes through a variety of landscapes from the marshy meadows near Bridger Lake, through a deep canyon and up a steep side canyon, to the Continental Divide on top of the Buffalo Plateau above timberline. I'd say that more folks come down the canyon than up the canyon. It sure is a lot easier that way.

Begin at Ferry Lake almost 10,000 feet high in the tundra. You get there by using Trails 11c, 11d, or 11b. There are two spurs to Woodard Pass (10,315 feet), on the Continental Divide. They both leave from Trail Number 11b, the Soda Fork Trail. The first spur is the more direct. It shoots off to the Divide at a sign about a third mile west of Ferry Lake. While more direct, this trail is also covered by a big snowdrift near the pass later in the year than the second spur. The second spur leaves a quarter mile east of Ferry Lake and ascends the 300 feet to the Continental Divide at a more leisurely pace.

On either route, snowdrifts sometimes prevent horse passage until after August 1, but backpackers can climb the snowdrifts.

Woodard Canyon, which the trail proceeds down, is very beautiful with rivulets from melting snow everywhere, surrounded by many alpine flowers in the tundra. Rising above the basin at the head

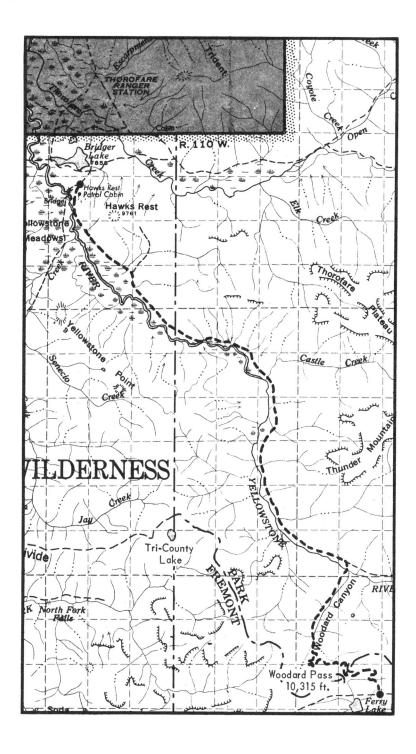

The canyon of the South Fork of the Yellowstone River.

of the canyon are volcanic rock walls with interesting contorted folds.

The trail follows several routes downward, and the grade becomes increasingly steep, at least until you reach a mid-canyon meadow. The grade then picks up once more, dropping 700 additional feet to a not-too-easy ford of the Yellowstone River. At the ford, you are in a deep canyon with volcanic rock walls rising vertically to near-vertically everywhere from 200 feet to 800 feet. Near the ford and especially above the ford (up-canyon on Trail Number 16a), there are some campsites, but as you move downstream the canyon's bottom narrows. The trail keeps about a hundred feet above the stream.

After about 2½ miles, the narrow canyon ends, although the trail remains above the river. Soon, you pass through a burn several decades old that started near the river and went all the way to timberline on Thunder Mountain, which forms the east wall of the canyon. Notice the dense reproduction of lodgepole pine. If there is a lot of seed on the ground during a fire, lodgepole will often grow back so densely that the little trees stagnate and never reach their potential height.

After you cross Castle Creek, the canyon broadens a great deal. The trail crosses the edge of a large meadow. Beginning about here, and continuing downstream, is very good moose habitat.

For two miles past this meadow the trail continues through a forest that grows on an ancient earthflow. Although the trailside itself is forested, the great Yellowstone Meadows have begun. All you have to do is cross the river to reach their upper end. The Yellowstone Meadows are nearly continuous from this point to ten miles downstream (well into Yellowstone Park). The entire area offers terrific fishing and fine wildlife habitat, and is also scenically beautiful.

Finally, the trail emerges from the forest and proceeds along the edge of the meadows at the base of Hawk's Rest Mountain to the Hawk's Rest Patrol Cabin and a trail junction.

Many rocky crags and alpine areas have been forever protected by our Wilderness system, but rarely has a great valley like the Upper Yellowstone been so fortunate. The valleys, of course, are always more productive of fish and wildlife than the mountains. It's too bad that some of the other great river valleys of the West were not kept in their natural state. The rarity of natural stream valleys, coupled with their great desirability, is what makes the Yellowstone Meadows the most crowded place in the Teton Wilderness. You might be tempted to complain that it is the classification as wilderness that

The South Fork of the Yellowstone from the Continental Divide.

Down Woodard Canyon from the Continental Divide.

makes the Upper Yellowstone popular, but I would disagree. If the
Forest Service hadn't had the foresight to set aside the Teton Wilderness in the 1930's, today a visitor to the Upper Yellowstone would
not be greeted by the sight of several pack-strings but rather by
thousands of cars and RV's. Despite its distance from present roads,
it would be easy to build a highway to the Upper Yellowstone. If
Wilderness classification didn't prevent it, you can bet that Wyoming
developers would have long ago insisted it be done.

16a   SOUTH FORK OF THE YELLOWSTONE

Length: 11½ miles.
Effort: 16½ miles from jct. of Trail Number
16 to Marston Pass; 12½ miles from
Marston Pass to jct. of Trail Number
16.
Trail condition: Fair to poor.
River crossings: Two.
Trail use: Very low.
Topographic Quadrangles: Ferry Lake,
Younts Peak.

The trail up the canyon of the South Fork of the Yellowstone
River is one of extraordinary beauty and scant use. It begins just the

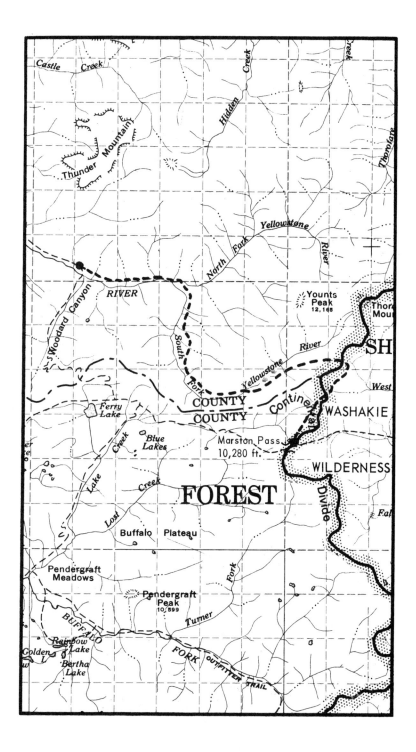

other side of the ford of the Yellowstone River at the bottom of Woodard Canyon. It goes upstream and into the South Fork of the Yellowstone, past mighty walls of convoluted volcanic rock, over the Continental Divide at 10,700 feet, and descends to Marston Pass on the edge of the Buffalo Plateau.

Most folks that come down Woodard Canyon head to Yellowstone Meadows. Usually they're interested in the fishing, and there are few fish in the Yellowstone River above a barrier (a small waterfall) a few miles past Castle Creek. The river looks great, but several plants in the past failed when the trout migrated downstream. Wyoming Game and Fish tried again in 1977, hopefully with better luck. Thus, only a few people travel upstream. If you like rugged mountain scenery, you should become one of these few.

For 2½ miles the trail follows the Yellowstone River, partly through timber and partly through meadow to the junction of this mighty river's north and south forks. The Yellowstone River is the longest undammed river in the lower 48 states (although coal companies are trying to correct this horrible situation).

A narrow meadow along the river offers places to camp and views of the plateau walls that rise 600 to 1000 feet nearly straight up on either side of the canyon above the forest. The North Fork of the Yellowstone is a deep and narrow-bottomed canyon with no trail. It originates at a small glacier on the north side of 12,156 foot high Younts Peak. The South Fork of the Yellowstone, by contrast, is a broad-bottomed canyon of lush meadows (although its side walls are equally as rugged as the North Fork's). The mouths of both forks are narrow and rugged.

Ford the North Fork a quarter mile above its mouth and climb through forest into the canyon of the South Fork. You struggle along a narrow trail on the canyon's sideslope for 1 ½ miles, crossing several tributary streams. Suddenly the trail descends into a beautiful, broad meadow. The South Fork of the Yellowstone meanders lazily, while tremendous plateau walls rise on each side of the meadow as well as ahead (due to the fact that the canyon bends).

Gradually the walls converge to squeeze the meadow into nonexistence. The trail follows the river closely for 1 ½ miles, then fords the river, climbs steeply, and gains 400 feet to emerge in the canyon's upper meadow. As the river tumbles from this meadow, it goes over a pretty waterfall (not on the maps).

The upper meadow is at timberline, and it is quite marshy. Flowers of all kinds bloom in August. It is possible to see elk or bighorn sheep.

The trail isn't good, but walking is easy (except for the dampness). You've got to find the route to Marston Pass, however, so you have to either find the trail or keep close to it. (After all you don't want to end up on a cliff in Younts Creek.) As you climb toward the head of the canyon past the meadow, you will see a low spot on the skyline with a mountain just to its right and a bigger mountain farther to its left. The big mountain is 12,058 foot Thorofare Mountain—second highest in the Wilderness. Don't go up there. It is the wrong pass. On the other side is the impassable Younts Creek. Instead, climb up the right side of the canyon wall and head for the lowest spot you can find. You come to a grassy divide. Just past this divide (indeed, it's the Continental Divide) there is a pond. Keep to the right and above the pond. Here you will find a trail contouring along the steep headwaters of West Fork Creek offering an incredible view! Circumnavigate the top of West Fork Creek and descend 400 feet to Marston Pass on the edge of the Buffalo Plateau. Here you join Trail Number 11c. You can either descend down Marston Creek into the Washakie Wilderness or go westward to Lake Creek or Ferry Lake. You should be aware that the traverse at the head of West Fork Creek requires an ice axe until late Summer.

17 ANGLES ENTRANCE

Length: 2½ miles.
Effort: 2½ miles from trailhead to the
*   South Buffalo River; 5½ miles from the*
*   South Buffalo back to the trailhead.*
Trail condition: Good.
River crossings: None.
Trail use: Heavy.
Topographic Quadrangle: Angle Mountain.

The Angles Trail is a rather short trail starting behind Togwotee Lodge (on U.S. 26/287) and dropping abruptly about 1600 feet to the South Fork of the Buffalo River. It provides quicker access to the South Buffalo Canyon than does Trail Number 11 which begins at Turpin Meadows. Of course, the quick access is on the way down. The hike back out is like hiking 5½ miles due to the steep climb.

Until a few years ago, this was an obscure trailhead—undeveloped—and the correct trail was a bit hard to find. Recently, the Forest Service improved the trailhead, made a parking place and put up a trail register. It's about the fourth busiest trailhead to the Teton Wilderness. This means you will usually find two or three cars parked there.

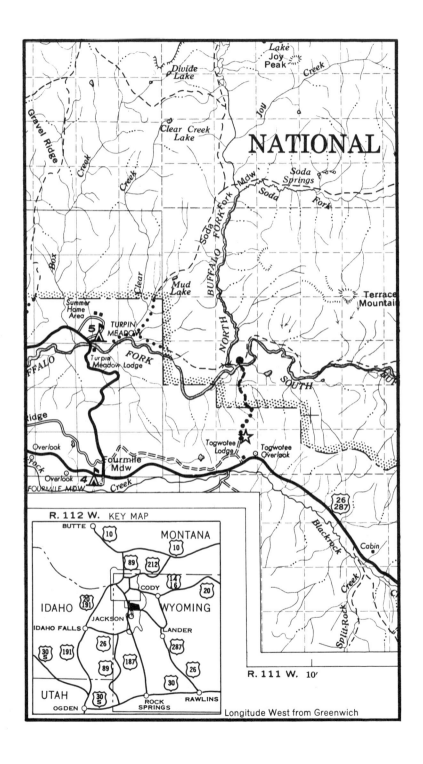

NATIONAL

Lake Joy Peak

Joy Creek

Divide Lake

Clear Creek Lake

Soda Springs

Mdw.

Soda

Soda Fork

SODA FORK

BUFFALO FORK

NORTH

Gravel Ridge

Creek

Creek

Box

Clear

Mud Lake

Summer Home Area

TURPIN MEADOW

Turpin Meadow Lodge

FORK

BUFFALO

Ridge

Overlook

Rock

Creek

Overlook

FOURMILE MDW

Fourmile Mdw

4

5

SOUTH

Terrace Mountain

Togwotee Lodge

Togwotee Overlook

Creek

26 287

Blackrock

Cabin

Split-Rock Creek

R. 112 W.   KEY MAP

BUTTE

10

MONTANA

10

89   212

114 16

CODY

20

IDAHO

20 191

JACKSON

WYOMING

IDAHO FALLS

LANDER

30 S   191

26

287

89   187

26

UTAH

30 S

OGDEN

ROCK SPRINGS

30

26

RAWLINS

R. 111 W.   10'

Longitude West from Greenwich

To reach the trailhead, drive to Togwotee Lodge which is about 17 miles east of Moran Junction on the highway to Dubois. Drive around to the back of the lodge taking the dirt road on the lodge's west side. You soon come to a dirt road leaving to the right (north). Take this road, and in about 1/5 mile the road ends at the trailhead.

The trail heads northward through forest and, appropriately, angles gradually over the shoulder of Angle Mountain. Then, after about ½ mile, the trail begins a steep switchbacking descent to the canyon of the South Buffalo.

The trail is mostly through forest, but just as you begin the steep part of the descent there is one magnificent view of the wilderness land lying before you to the north. Spread out for your pleasure and inspiration is the canyon of the South Buffalo, the North Buffalo, Terrace Mountain and other wilderness attractions. Ponder the fact that northward from here there is not another road for about fifty miles as the crow flies. It's further than fifty miles by trail.

After completing its steep decline to the canyon bottom, the trail crosses the South Buffalo on a good bridge (suitable for pack stock) and joins with the South Buffalo River Trail on the river's north side.

Quite a few fishermen come down this trail on day hikes for the good fishing in the river. They usually struggle the 1600 feet back up under the weight of some nice catches, although there are getting to be too many whitefish in the river. The camping is good near the bottom of the trail along the river.

This concludes the description of the trails of the Teton Wilderness, but it isn't a complete description of this piece of wildland, for there are opportunities for hundreds of cross country hikes to places beautiful and rarely seen. Most are not difficult. I leave them for you to discover.

Epilogue

The wilds now protected in the Teton Wilderness have existed without man's help or interference for millions of years. The promise of the Wilderness Act is that man will not destroy these wild places. This promise, however, is a political promise. Even though the Teton Wilderness and the other gems in the National Wilderness Preservation System are protected by Congress, Congress can repeal, amend, or water-down anything it has previously done. The President and the Secretary of the Interior also have the authority, via some loopholes in the Wilderness Act, to order Wilderness areas leased for oil, gas, and other minerals. Even as this is being written, the oil companies are asking that the Teton Wilderness and the great Bob Marshall Wilderness in Montana be leased to explore and develop any oil or gas that may lie under the earth. Never in the past has any such raid on the Wilderness System been attempted—and the statements of President Reagan indicate that he means to allow it.

To many of us, wilderness is sacred. It means freedom. Freedom to come and go at will without asking permission, freedom to seek beauty, adventure, to face danger on our own terms, and overcome it. Wilderness is a place where the State doesn't rule us. We rule ourselves and benefit or suffer directly from our choices.

Most estimates are that all of the oil that may exist under the Teton Wilderness would not supply the nation's demand for more than a few days. Thus we must ask, "What is the real reason they want to destroy the wilderness?" Could it be that the giant businesses and their friends in government fear the freedom of the wilderness—a freedom that gives us a different vision than what they would manufacture for us?

The Teton Wilderness will remain wild only so long as we are vigilant. Otherwise, these ancient mountains may have fewer years left to their life than we mortals to ours.

Index

182